StyleCity
AMSTERDAM

StyleCity
AMSTERDAM

With over 400 color photographs and 6 maps

Thames & Hudson

Contents

Street Wise

Style Traveller

Series concept and editor: Lucas Dietrich
Jacket and book design: Grade Design Consultants
Original design and map concept: The Senate
Maps: Peter Bull

Research and texts: Sian Tichar
Specially commissioned photography by
Anthony Webb

Although every effort has been made to ensure that
the information in this book is as up-to-date and as
accurate as possible at the time of going to press,
some details are liable to change.

First published in paperback in the United States of
America in 2004 by Thames & Hudson Inc., 500 Fifth
Avenue, New York, New York 10110

thamesandhudsonusa.com

Library of Congress Catalog Card Number 2003113655
ISBN 0-500-21009-8

Sian Tichar would like to thank the Netherlands Board
of Tourism UK & Ireland (www.holland.com/uk) and
Nederlandse Spoorwegen for their generous assistance.

Printed in China by C & C Offset Printing Co Ltd

How to Use This Guide

The book features two principal sections: **Street Wise** and **Style Traveller**.

Street Wise, which is arranged by neighbourhood, features areas that can be covered in a day (and night) on foot and includes a variety of locations – cafés, shops, restaurants, museums, performance spaces, bars – that capture local flavour or are lesser-known destinations.

The establishments in the **Style Traveller** section represent the city's best and most characteristic locations – 'worth a detour' – and feature hotels (**sleep**), restaurants (**eat**), cafés and bars (**drink**), boutiques and shops (**shop**) and getaways (**retreat**).

Each location is shown as a circled number on the relevant neighbourhood map, which is intended to provide a rough idea of location and proximity to major sights and landmarks rather than precise position. Locations in each neighbourhood are presented sequentially by map number. Each entry in the **Style Traveller** has two numbers: the top one refers to the page number of the neighbourhood map on which it appears; the second number is its location.

For example, the visitor might begin by selecting a hotel from the **Style Traveller** section. Upon arrival, **Street Wise** might lead him to the best joint for coffee before guiding him to a house-museum nearby. After lunch he might go to find a special jewelry store listed in the **shop** section. For a memorable dining experience, he might consult his neighbourhood section to find the nearest restaurant crossreferenced to **eat** in **Style Traveller**.

Street addresses are given in each entry, and complete information – including email and web addresses – is listed in the alphabetical **contact** section. Travel and contact details for the destinations in **retreat** are given at the end of **contact**.

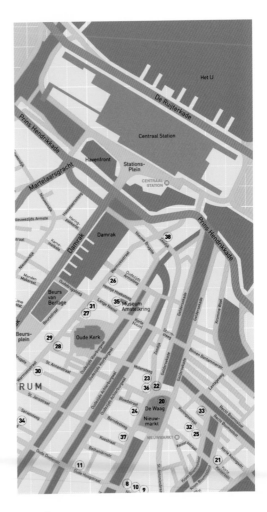

Legend

②	Location
■	Museums, sights
■	Gardens, squares
Ⓜ	Metro stops
▬	Streets

AMSTERDAM

Like the diamonds that are famously polished there, Amsterdam has many facets. It is this versatility that is key to the passion the city evokes in its more than 700,000 inhabitants and over twice that number of annual visitors. Its layers are a reflection of the country for which it is the social and economic – if not political – capital. In the 17th century, during the period referred to as its Golden Age, Amsterdam was the greatest trading city in the world. And the Netherlands remains a supremely powerful nation – it owns the electronics giant Philips and shares Unilever and Shell with the Brits. Yet you would be forgiven for not being familiar with the origins of these global corporations, as one of the country's other assets is its Calvinist-imbued modesty when it comes to cultural achievements, a virtue recognized by Simon Schama in his 1987 study of the Dutch nation, *The Embarrassment of Riches*. The Dutch embody the pragmatic, long-term view with regard to socio-economic developments: industrial, even architectural, decisions are all weighted by an awareness that finances trough and peak.

The city also has a rich colonial past, apparent from the Indonesian, Surinamese and, more recently, southern African flavours found in the multi-cultural cooking pot that has evolved in Amsterdam quarters and kitchens. As an affluent northern European city with a medieval heart that is largely intact, it is an attractive destination for settlers from around the world (but its tolerance means that by no stretch of the imagination are they all from developing countries); members of a total of 173 nationalities have chosen Amsterdam as their home. The trail to Sin City is trodden by millions who associate Amsterdam with legalized prostitution and dope-selling coffeeshops. Unbeknown to the sex tourists – and luckily for the local population – the outlets providing these gratifications are confined to small Disney-esque (thanks to the red neon alerting their presence) sectors, so it is entirely possible to live in the city and rarely encounter its underbelly. Of course, the art of compromise is such that these wares are on offer should they be required, and the ensuing social implications are – as much as possible – structured and monitored by a political system that realizes recognition of an industry renders it taxable. In fact, tax is the big leveller in the Netherlands and the highest strata will remove 55 per cent from a salary. This is why public transport runs so efficiently, why streets are clean, why the city is rich in public art and monuments and why there is so much social growth and new architecture on the fringes of the suburbs. Of course, most funding nowadays is private, but the leftist awareness that has been at the heart of decades of Dutch politics pervades many levels of lifestyle and answers many a *buitenlander*'s (foreigner's) question about how the Dutch have managed to engage in such a practical evolution.

Only through centuries of rigorous social planning has Amsterdam evolved into the series of neighbourhoods that form it today. Each has its own beguiling characteristics and resident type. The Dutch frequently complain about their excessive population density (the highest in Europe), but the 165 canals that encircle and intersect Amsterdam prevent claustrophobia from ever really setting in. The healthy attitude to getting around (there are 400,000 bicycles in Amsterdam alone) using, wherever possible, car- and pedestrian-free *fietspads* (cycle paths) is another enterprising method of harmonious existence, rather than compromise, in a very small city.

The Dutch love for *gezellig* ('cosy, convivial') socializing is celebrated across the city in its 755 restaurants and almost 1,500 cafés and bars, in which style mirrors the tastes of a local population, hungry to perform on the international stages of architecture and design. Certain architects (of construction and ideas), Sjoerd Soeters, C&D Dam, MVRDV, Droog & Co, Concrete, Merx&Girod, B. Inc Interior Stuff, FG Stijl, keep cropping up again and again as the visual candy craftsmen of the ever more – choose applicable adjective – glamorous/mature/low-key/cosy/designer hotels, bars, restaurants and shops that are opening up city-wide. Their performances are directly attributable to the growing prosperity of proprietors who own several *horeca* establishments (a Dutch neologism that encompasses 'hotel', 'restaurant' and 'café').

The socializing behaviour of Amsterdam has been forged by a few crucial personalities whose names form the basis of the creative pages of an Amsterdam *Who's Who*. These stories are mapped by their own tastes and desires and those of their maturing contemporaries, which have evolved from theatrical party-performances in crazy clubs and taking art outside of the white cube to shoving it right back in again and dining in hidden eateries. Through it all, these design adventures are accompanied by a laid-back sense of humour, a tone intrinsic to Amsterdam. The resulting quality shared by all the store/*horeca*/gallery owners is the belief in taking a simple idea and having the tenacity to develop it for mass consumption, yet all the while maintaining its existence in the village-like structure of the city. Visitors seeking culture, decadence, glamorous nightlife or an exploration of liberal socialism will not be disappointed. Amsterdam's ability to satiate desire, however extraordinary, is unsurpassed.

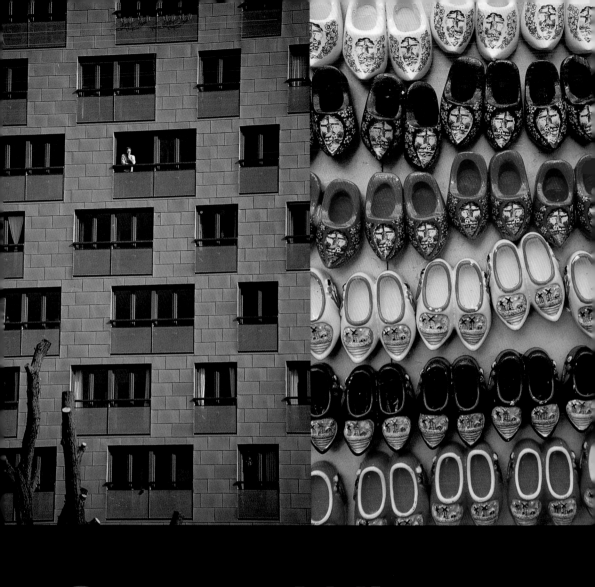

Street Wise

Nieuwe Centrum
Oude Centrum

The heart of the city is divided into *het oude zijde* (the old side) and *het nieuwe zijde* (the new side), which, dating back to medieval times, is not actually new at all. The two are spliced by the neon nightmare of the Damrak, which cuts a straight line south to the Dam where it changes name, though not direction, and becomes the Rokin, ending at the Muntplein intersection of the floating flower market and a corner of the chaotic Rembrandtplein.

Flanked by the Koninklijk Paleis (royal palace) and 600-year-old Nieuwe Kerk (new church) on one side and the premier Dutch department store De Bijenkorf and Hotel Krasnapolsky on the other, the Dam Square has long been a convergence point for tourists. The sit-ins there parallel the love that locals have for sitting outdoors, something that you witness on any sunny day in the city, as people drag sofas from their homes to the street outside, from where they enjoy a drink and the view.

The older eastern side requires rose-tinted vision from visitors, as it is here that you will find an X-rated 'Disneyland' in the alleys of the infamous red-light district, which wind from the base of Amsterdam's oldest church, Oude Kerk. This vice sector represents the epitome of the tolerance for which Amsterdam is so admired, and a cavalier attitude prevails from all but ogling tourists towards the windows where women boldly flaunt their wares. In fact, the red-light district and some of the oldest streets in the city – the Zeedijk (where the jazz trumpeter Chet Baker fell to a heroin-induced death in 1988) and the Warmoesstraat (once the playground of prostitutes and drug dealers) – have undergone facelifts thanks to recent investment in street repavement and clean-up projects. This is slowly encouraging hip bars and boutiques to appear sporadically between the coffeeshops (selling marijuana), headshops (which sell the tools with which to roll and smoke it) and sex shops that dominate this part of town.

The centre is also home to the scattered complex of Amsterdam University, and the cafés frequented by its students are some of the best in town. The Staalstraat's popular use as a shoot location for such notorious films as Dutch horror movie *Amsterdamned* is only a clue to how delightful and diverse the range of shops and eateries along and around this little street are.

The newer side, to the west of the Damrak, features Amsterdam's main pedestrian shopping street. The Kalverstraat has an identical twin in every town in the country, all of which feature outlets of the same generic Dutch shops on a similarly pedestrianized street. It is the artery streets of this area that need exploration, rather than the heart.

1   Nieuwezijds Voorburgwal

- Diep Venue, no. 256
- BEP, no. 260
- Absinthe, no. 171
- NL Lounge, no. 169

Located a convenient stumble from one another are some of Amsterdam's best late-night watering holes. They vary in style and – to a degree – in clientele, but have remained popular with the maturing and loyal Amsterdam crowd that has been knocking 'em back in these bars since Diep Venue was first opened by Frank Traas and Rob Zorab (who recently opened Suite [p. 146]) in 1996. The bar is legendary and throws regular parties, but is a no-frills, masculine, spirit-swigging local. BEP has the most contemporary décor and serves sushi-style snacks. It belongs to Waldy Brewster, who also named his café across the street after his sister and co-proprietor Delores. Until recently, absinthe was subject to a global ban because of its link with brain damage (in fact, it was blamed for Van Gogh's ear-cutting incident). But it is now freely available at the eponymous bar. The NL Lounge was for a while the hippest club in town, with queues outside to prove it. It remains, like all these venues, occasionally hard to get into.

STRANGERS IN THE NIGHT

2   Supperclub

151

SWING LOW SWEET CHARIOT

3   Suite

146

ORGANIC SHACK CHIC

4   Delores

Nieuwezijds Voorburgwal

Delores and Waldy Brewster are keeping it in the family with her café located opposite his bar, BEP, on the Nieuwezijds Voorburgwal. Her funky café appears as a converted newspaper stand on an island in the middle of the road. Despite this, most of the seating is outside and the lure of quality, all-organic fare keeps her even busier than the traffic passing by. Organic products are gaining ground in the Netherlands and Delores's home-made burgers, sandwiches and juices stand testimony to the popularity of the health-conscious movement. If anyone is in doubt, the final word in restaurant critiquing in the Netherlands comes from Johannes van Dam of *Het Parool*, who gives her a rating of 9 out of 10: read 'outstanding'.

GA-GA-ISM

5   Baby

Nieuwezijds Voorburgwal 262

René Eller gave birth to Baby some five years ago and it is growing fast. Baby is a design agency, art gallery, studio and magazine. Eller had previously filled a cathedral-sized church on the Keizersgracht with a private Baby club featuring exhibitions and a meeting place. But he decided to get bigger on an international scale and smaller locally, so recently moved into an office and gallery space surrounded by the bars of Nieuwezijds Voorburgwal. Eller's background as an international music video director places him in a central position to connect people/themes as they occur in the major media-savvy cities. His current project will see him open more Baby galleries in 15 cities around the world. Watch this (ground-floor gallery) space.

DRY CLEAN ONLY

6   Laundry Industry

Spuistraat 137 (Magna Plaza)

Since 1992, Willem Masser and Ellen Steenbeek have been selling functional fashion under the Laundry Industry label. In the early days they supplied only wholesale clothing and had to wash all the cotton garments themselves. When they were ready to set up shop on their own, they took the name as a humorous reflection of the less glamorous side of the fashion production process. Masser and Steenbeek share their work, with Steenbeek controlling the creative design of the label and Masser masterminding the brand and business. They have three outlets in Amsterdam selling their timeless functional fashion, Magna Plaza, Rokin and Van Baerlestraat.

SOBRIETY AND SANCTUARY

7   Spui Book Market and the Begijnhof

Spui

Spui was once the meeting point of journalists, writers and intellectuals from the Spuistraat. As with London's Fleet Street, the papers and writers have moved on, but every Friday an antiquarian book market is hosted in the paved square. The nearby secluded, foliage-lush courtyard of the Begijnhof (built in 1346 for a devout Catholic sisterhood) is well worth a visit. Amsterdam's oldest surviving house (1475) is also located here at no. 34, while at the southern section stands the Englese Kerk built for the 'Begijntjes' in 1419. Now the well-kept gardens and sanctuary are ideal for anyone seeking a moment of inner-city calm.

8 Puck

Nieuwe Hoogstraat 1a

Puck was a pale and sober outlet for vintage wedding dresses until Elena and her daughter Pascale Bunink got their playful little mitts on it in 2000 and infused contemporary and colourful fashion design into the joint. The split mezzanine level store showcases two members of the Dutch fashion movement in the form of High Cue (who make high-waisted, Marlene Dietrich-style pants) and Anne-Claire Petit: red raffia straw floral-print baglets and smock-topped Chinese pyjama outfits (for children and adults). You can still find antique kimonos, bedspreads and shams, but the dusty sexiness is balanced by the vitality of Helena Christensen's Bruun's Bazaar label and Noa Noa.

9 A. Boeken

Nieuwe Hoogstraat 31

The Boeken family have run this haberdashery shop since 1920 on the busy tourist drag that is the Hoogstraat. Currently under the control of André Boeken, it is one of several 'finds' on an otherwise pizza-/shawarma-seller-strewn street. Spread across three shops, defined by their camp red canopy, Boeken is stuffed to bursting with rolls and bales of fabric. Shelves and cupboards are crammed with buttons, zips, tapes, lace, cords, ruffs and feathers. Equally a couturier's and a transvestite's dream, Boeken claims the most extensive choice in Europe of latex and artificial leather, coupled with a rainbow of fake fur in every length and animal print known to man. And woman.

GO FLY A KITE
10 Joe's Vliegerwinkel
Nieuwe Hoogstraat 19

SPICE IT UP
11 Capsicum
Oude Hoogstraat 1

'Joe' is not a bloke, but the abbreviation of Joint Overseas Enterprises, a nifty name that the original owners came up with for their kite shop (*vliegerwinkel*) some 30 years ago. Today the shop is in the hands of owners Willy Staats and Jolanda Markus, who have given the running of it over to the expert kite builder Martijn de Vries. His passion for kites is infectious, and he is only too happy to explain the difference between static-line (for kids) and dual-line (necessary for precision flying) varieties. From there you distinguish the power kites that will sustain the velocity for beach buggies or board-surfing and pattern-flying kites that paint shapes in the sky. The *vliegerwinkel* has them all, plus base materials – poles, fabric and parts – to build your own.

Punning playfully on the fact that their last name is Pepper, husband-and-wife team Steve and Deborah opened Capsicum almost 30 years ago. The American couple transplanted to the Netherlands via India, where Deborah succumbed to an obsession for textiles. This is apparent even from outside the store, where transparent glass windows reveal huge folded fabric bales and resemble an oversized material library. All cloths and soft furnishings are designed and styled in the Netherlands by the couple or by local talent. One such is Mariette Wolbert, whose creativity has been stitched out in a double weave with a loop in contrasting coloured threads.

BOOK TRADE
12 Oudemanhuispoort
Oudemanhuispoort

Stumbling across this slim covered walkway that joins
the Oudezijds Achterburgwal and the Kloveniersburgwal
will prove deeply satisfying to those who love inner-city
secrets. The Oudemanhuispoort was once the entrance for
'old people's almshouses' and was built in 1754. Now part
of Amsterdam University, the building is closed to the
public, but you can still observe the pediment over the
gateway on the Oudezijds Achterburgwal, which depicts
a pair of reading glasses, an indicator of 'old age'. The
arcade remains public domain and the sensibilities of the
historical shopper will also be appeased: there has been
trading inside this covered walkway since 1757. Today it
is a market for second-hand books.

CHOCOLATE OPERA
13 Puccini Bomboni
 164

MUSHROOM MANIA
14 Innerspace
Staalstraat 5

Meila Schot has two stores in Amsterdam selling magic
mushrooms. The current legal status in Holland is that
fresh mushrooms are legal, but any dried variety is not.
Innerspace sells its mushrooms packaged from a
refrigerated cabinet. They are imported from Thailand,
Ecuador and Colombia for a hallucinogenic high and from
Mexico for a more mellow trip. The 'smart store' advocates
natural highs and also sells truffles, San Pedro cactus and
peyote. These shops are unique to Holland and attempt to
provide educated, informed advice for users of natural
mood-enhancing drugs.

FOOD FOR THE PEOPLE
15 Café de Jaren
 134

DRY DESIGN, HOT IDEAS
16 Droog & Co
 154

17 Juggle Store
Staalstraat 3

The Englishman David Marchant and his Dutch wife Anne van Raaij toured Europe in the early 1980s with their magic, juggling and movement show. They found props hard to find on the road and had to make their own. Requests for the balls and beanbags grew, and they ran a wholesale business until opening the Juggle Store in 1996. Clubs, diabolos, beanbags, yo-yos, devil sticks, unicycles, rings, glow-in-the-dark sticks and juggling scarves are just some of the circus tools they provide. Marchant makes his own balls and recently launched a bouncing silicone variety.

ART BOOK
18 Nijhof & Lee
Staalstraat 13a

A specialist international bookstore trading in- and out-of-print books, especially art, architecture, design and photography. Further emphasis is placed on typography, exhibition catalogues, reference works and graphic design. Recently, they have developed a growing collection of posters by Dutch graphic designers from the second half of the 20th century. Many are by master typographer Wim Crouwel, who was responsible during the 1960s and 1970s for posters, catalogues and exhibitions at the Stedelijk before becoming director of the seminal Boijmans Van Beuningen museum in the 1980s. A small collection of limited editions by artists is also available here.

COFFEESHOP
19 Rusland
Rusland 14–16

A coffeeshop in Amsterdam is not really somewhere to go to sip a latte or mochaccino. Here is where you can buy marijuana and find a mellow place in which to enjoy a smoke. If you want to experience a coffeeshop, Rusland ('Russia'), named after the street it is on, is a more mature place than most others, which tend to attract only tourists. There are cushions for lounging on the floor and the usual gangja bar where you make a selection from an extensive menu. The choice comes down to preference, as each variety provides a different type of high, ranging from peaceful and contemplative to giggly and all-out hallucinatory.

WEIGHING HOUSE
20 In de Waag
Nieuwmarkt 4

Amsterdam's old weighing house could be a less camp version of Sleeping Beauty's castle. Its turreted structure deserves more attention than the taxi ranks and overcrowded bar terraces of the Nieuwmarkt that surround it. In de Waag began life as St Antoniespoort in 1488, a gate defending the city wall. In 1617 it was the place where all wholesale goods were weighed for taxes and thus the square became a hive of trading activity. Later in the century the south tower was used by the Guild of Surgeons as a dissecting room and the bricklayers guild met there too. Other less imaginative cities may have enshrined such history in a museum, but In de Waag is a buzzy restaurant with an up-to-date menu. The interior still manages to retain a stylized dark medieval cosiness.

LOCAL
21 Café 't Hoekje
Krom Boomssloot 47

Only a block away from the debris of the Nieuwmarkt, this 'café on the corner' is a sweet secret to all but the locals who drink and dine here. It is run by a collective of five women ('oh, no one wants to know our last names, do they?'). Barbara, Fifine, Nancy, Bobby and Betty all knew one another and shared a desire for a bar that would also serve affordable home-made fare. This corner has housed a bar since the 1930s, and the tiny Art Déco stained-glass interior was 'updated' in the 1950s with some wild neon. It still screams *gezellig* (the unique Dutchism for a good time with cosy friends). Betty and Nancy cook at home and bring in delicious hummus and lamb meatballs with mint yoghurt and even bake their own cakes.

CRAZY DUTCH
22 Latei
Zeedijk 143

David Klinkert acquired Latei in 1999 and decorated it with the help of Nina Jokinen and a plethora of artifacts collected from flea markets and dusty second-hand shops. Everything is for sale, including the furniture and crockery. Klinkert is constantly replacing or adding to his hoard in the mini café, which serves wholesome meals, home-baked bread, damn good coffee and fresh organic juices. The hotchpotch organic approach to running a café has resulted in spontaneous events, limbo night or 'bring, play – and then sell – your own records' night.

AND LEMON DISCO

23 Lime
Zeedijk 104

Richard Klerk took a big risk when he opened a retro bar on the crummy Zeedijk in 1999. At the time, the old street was a mess of Chinese restaurants, drug addicts and old-school brown bars. His tiny cocktail lounge inspired by the 1960s and 1970s stood out like a sore thumb. But following the opening of the Buddhist temple (p. 29) and a facelift in the form of new paving, Zeedijk is finally emerging from its seedy skin. Klerk has filled the bar with furniture he designed himself based on 1960s classics and made up by Houtwerk, the custom furniture makers of Beeverwijk. The walls sport 1970s graphics and now-kitsch photos of Aruba beach life. Glamour is added to the mix via the sparkling mirror reflections of a disco ball.

GOING NATIVE
24 Lokaal 't Loosje
Nieuwmarkt 32–34

The word *lokaal* is Dutch for 'room' and, when featured as part of the name of a bar, is customarily attached to the word *proef*, indicating a tasting room. This bar once had a function as a waiting room, when trams used to run through the Nieuwmarkt. Today the *lokaal* refers only to the choice of beers and spirits, which is vast and attracts all the local market stall holders and drinkers thanks to its refreshing lack of pretension, away from the tourist bustle and taxi ranks that dominate the square. But Loosje is noisy, brash and full of laughter: there is always a crowd at the bar. It is a great place to sample local brews and convivial Dutch conversation.

BACKSTREET BOLT-HOLE
25 Eetcafe van Beeren
Koningsstraat 54

Only a block away from the chaos of Nieuwmarkt is a brown café so delightful, original and peaceful that drinkers would be forgiven for thinking they were in a country village. This idea is intensified by the private garden out back, which is embellished with flowers, herbs (also used in the classic French cuisine served here) and trees. Herbert Hofthazer was cooking here for six years before he took full control in 2001. The café remains pleasantly immune to the hectic world just a street away: no music, no phones and the only decoration being art works with which a penniless drinking artist used to pay his bar bill two decades ago.

26 Getto

Warmoesstraat 51

This camp kitsch bar opened its doors in 1996 as a place to be enjoyed by all – gay, bisexual, lesbian and straight – and it is exactly this 'anything goes' attitude that keeps the non-gay-friendly crowd out. You are as likely to see a group of leather-clad queens toasting over a bottle of champagne as you are lesbians having their fortunes told on the occasional theme evenings. Groups of straight friends meet here as well, and it is worth heading through the bar to the restaurant at the back. The menu is surprisingly reasonable, the portions huge and wholesome. It is a very 'sweet' space, where there is always a friendly smile from the staff or someone to talk to at the glittery bar.

THE BAKER'S SHOP

27 De Bakkerswinkel

ART HOTEL

28 Winston

COFFEE BEAN, TEA LEAF

29 Wijs & Zonen

SQUAT ART

30 W139

Warmoesstraat 139

When they first squatted this building in 1979, the collective of artists had little idea that some 24 years later they would be commemorating their position as one of Amsterdam's most cutting-edge spaces in a 383-page retrospective volume. Back then, the Warmoesstraat was an undesirable, derelict backstreet, but the artists were pleased to find a usable production house in which to exhibit raw art. After someone fell through the ceiling during one of the infamous rambunctious openings, the staff and volunteers took on caretaking roles and started to restore the space. This restoration has recently shifted up a few gears and W139 are temporarily moving out so that the building can be transformed under the experienced eye of Sjoerd Soeters (who is responsible for much of the architecture on the Eilanden), Vincent Smulders and Bob van Reeth.

COFFEE AND TEA

31 Geels & Co

Warmoesstraat 67

For five generations the Geels family have built up their selection of teas, which now number nearly 100 varieties. The business is in the hands of Esther Geel, who is the first female in the family to hold the responsibility. Teas and the requisite brewing equipment are sold from the pleasantly old-fashioned store, and all purchases can be tasted, measured and sampled before a final choice is made. The tea selection ranges from traditional Ceylon and Assam to rarer Gen Maichi and Pai Mu Tan and is complemented by a range of over 20 coffees.

FURNITURE

32 Metri

Koningsstraat 36

Jaap van Duyvendijk has been designing and consulting on interiors as Metri for 25 years. He provides the 'stuff that surrounds you' via furniture, kitchens and offices. Metri was inspired by the Metro stop next door, and the metric aspect of his made-to-measure designs (the business was started as a group effort but only van Duyvendijk remains). A recent design experiment in lamp making – red fairy flowers that grew from a silver stem – was a 'little joke', but thanks to its popularity (he had left it lying out in the studio-store), he now admits, 'I am willing to sell my jokes'.

ARE YOU SITTING COMFORTABLY?

33 Zitzo

Krom Boomssloot 4a

Zitzo is a Dutch colloquialism for a comfortable seat. Edward Postma opened his showroom selling chairs, lights and other pieces of furniture in July 2000. His background was arguably the antithesis to 20th-century design classics; he worked in construction before several years in finance. During this time he gradually built up a vast collection of classic design pieces, reflected in the selection in the store. Pieces by Ray and Charles Eames, Arne Jacobsen and Verner Panton are spread over three floors of the German architect Han Slawick's old studio and are available to rent as well as to buy.

TASTING HOUSE

34 Wynand Fockink

166

In 1578, following the Reformation, Amsterdam became officially Protestant, and Catholics were forbidden to worship openly. For Jan Hartman this meant private prayer, and in 1661 he converted the top floors of his 17th-century canal house into a secret chapel. It is an astonishing addition to the house, which is also home to the only remaining original parlour room in the city. There is also a pastry café where visitors can ponder the past over a succulent *appeltaart*.

True to the egalitarianism for which Holland is famed, Her Majesty Queen Beatrix became the first state figure to publicly support Buddhism when she opened the largest temple in Europe built in traditional Chinese palace style in 2000. The Fo Guang Shan 'He Hua' Temple comes as a visual shock. It is built on the seedy Zeedijk and, despite the municipality's attempts to clean up the area, remains an anomaly. Perhaps such incongruity is at the very heart of the faith.

Peter Oldenboom is the seventh generation of his family to run this natural-remedy drugstore since it was founded in 1743 by Jacob Hooy. The selection has changed little over the years and herbs, spices and homeopathic remedies are sold from the wooden barrels and boxes stacked floor to ceiling behind the original serving counter. The air is pungent with the herbs, but sharper still is Holland's best-loved treat: the *dropje*, or liquorice drop. Eaten by young and old, supplied in every possible shape and variation, the *dropjes* are on view in old glass sweet jars.

tike
design
FOOTSTOOLS

10 stuks € 5,-
2 bos € 8.50

40 Knuffels

Sint Antoniesbreestraat 39–51

One of the Dutch nation's more unusual obsessions is its love of stuffed toy animals. At Knuffels they believe that northern Europeans have an affinity for animals, which is reflected in their extensive collections of soft toys. Whatever the reason, this is not the only store in Amsterdam dedicated to Furbies (although it does claim to have the craziest and scariest), but it redeems itself by housing the city's largest clog-selling outlet in its basement, which is also part of the Metro system. Bruno Jonker has been making clogs for more than 20 years and is happy to demonstrate how he carves the pointed and round-toe varieties (the former used by fishermen to step on their nets, the latter by farmers to tread through soil).

FOOTSTOOLS PLUS
41 Tike Design

Grimburgwal 15

Tike Veenstra opened Tike Design in 2002 in response to the growing demand for her footstools, which had only been available in galleries, craft fairs and 'guest appearances' in other shops. Originally trained in fashion design and working as a milliner in the *hautes chapeaux* salon of Peter Voorn, Tike was inspired by the vision that a footstool is much more than just a low bench on four legs. Testimony to this is her tiny outlet, fit to bursting with unique footstools upholstered in kaleidoscopic fabrics or luminous plastics, with cow-bone or wooden legs collected from around the globe.

DRINKS AWAY!
42 Kapitein Zeppos

145

CIGAR CITY
43 PGC Hajenius

162

FLOATING FLOWERS
44 Bloemenmarkt

Singel between Muntplein & Koningsplein

The idea of a flower market on water is enough to make this part of any visitor's Amsterdam itinerary, but the canal barges are such permanent structures, docked firmly to the canal side, that the floating aspect gets a little lost in this stretch of the Singel. Yet there is rarely disappointment in terms of choice, colour and price. The plant sellers take full advantage of the local flowers and bulbs that are available all year round. The art of crossbreeding has developed over centuries and has evolved astounding varieties (red petals bleeding into mauve backgrounds, tulips that are so purple they are almost black). Taken close to the source, ferns, palms, geraniums, indoor cypresses, orchids, roses, carnations, pansies and seeds and bulbs to plant at home are relatively inexpensive.

TIT FOR TAT
45 Waterlooplein

Waterlooplein

Dating back to 1882, when two canals were filled in to provide the market square for the Jewish quarter, Waterlooplein is dominated by the town hall and Stadhuis Muziektheater, home of the Nationale Ballet and the Nederlands Opera and host to visiting guest productions ranging from rock to rococo. It is colloquially called the 'Stopera' (an amalgamation of 'Stadhuis' and 'Opera') and combines its cultural function with public duties. Since it was built in 1987, it has been at the receiving end of a perhaps disproportionate amount of criticism. There are witty thought-provoking ornaments in the architecture in the form of transparent tubes that indicate sea-level, reminding observers that Holland is predominantly below this watermark. Zero point, the marker from which heights in much of Europe are calculated, is located here. In front of the theatre is a market selling second-hand and new clothes, bric-à-brac and even bikes (note: the really cheap ones are probably stolen).

West
Jordaan
Haarlemmerbuurt

While the grand canal rings were under construction in the 17th century, the city planner Hendrick Staets was setting out the marshland beyond the Prinsengracht as a home for workers and immigrants fleeing religious or political persecution (Protestants from the southern Netherlands and France, Jews from Poland, Portugal and Germany, Pilgrim Fathers from England). The network of streets and canals runs along the natural courses of drainage ditches and cart paths and forms the modern-day Jordaan. Huguenot refugees referred to the district with its many *hofjes* (almshouses built around courtyard gardens) as *le jardin* (the garden). There is debate over whether this word forms the base of the area's name today or whether it derives from the Dutch word *joden*, meaning Jewish, for the refugee group who resided there. Alongside the *hofjes*, the Jordaan is famed for its *bruine cafés* ('brown cafés') or pubs with characteristic brownish hues (from the décor and tobacco-stained walls), whose quaint interiors are quintessentially *gezellig*, a necessary quality among the Dutch.

Today, the Jordaan is a hip 'hood and home to the young, upwardly mobile middle-class Amsterdam set. Unlike in much of the rest of the city, its streets are not focused around huge monuments and it retains a small-scale, genuinely residential neighbourhood feel. If there is a nucleus to these streets then it is probably found at the Noordermarkt, which hosts an enticing farmers' market on Saturdays and where adjoining streets hide some of the city's most controversial contemporary art galleries.

Just north of the Noordermarkt lies the original supply route to Haarlem on the Haarlemmerstraat and Haarlemmerdijk. Like many other now über-fashionable stretches in the city, this was the stomping ground of squatters who occupied its buildings during the 1980s and early 1990s. New money and new life have transformed it into boutique heaven. Its western-most tip is marked by the unmissable city gate, the Haarlemmerport, built in 1840 but previously a defended gateway that opened the bustling road to Haarlem. Today it stands as a pointer towards one of the city's largest ongoing cultural projects on the site of a former gas factory, the Westergasfabriek (p. 37). Thirteen listed buildings and acres of disused land form the site, which after years of reconstruction recently opened as a complex of public parks, artists' studio spaces, a theatre and music venue and a sports ground, adding a dynamic element to the city's activities and reinventing an industrial wasteland as Amsterdam's latest cultural destination.

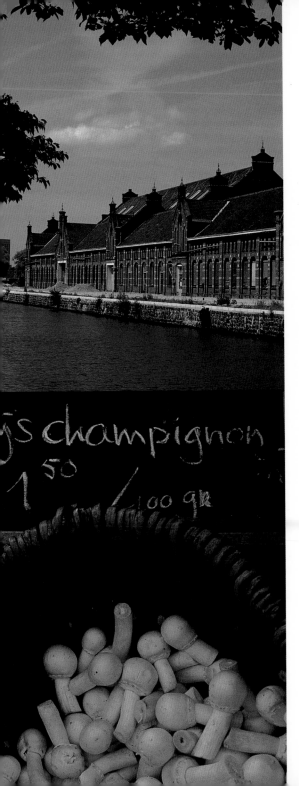

1 Westergasfabriek

Haarlemmerweg 8–10

Just west of Amsterdam's centre is the city's foremost multimedia cultural centre. The site buildings of the old gas factory (which fuelled the city's street lamps in the 19th century) were listed as historic monuments and renovation took place around them. The culture park was designed and laid out by the American landscape artist Kathryn Gustafson and, although the park was completed only at the end of 2003, project manager Evert Verhagen opened the buildings in 1992 to host the Holland and Drum Rhythm Festivals, as well as a continuing party of DJs and live performances. Now that the park has been enhanced by picnic lawns, tennis courts and a huge reed pond, the project is focusing on the buildings themselves. One is already home to the leading theatre company Toneel Groep Amsterdam, which continues to present shows there. The undertaking is an inspirational example of metamorphosis from a defunct, polluted inner-city space to a cultural hot spot that attracts patronage on an international scale.

MEDIEVAL MARKET

2 Noordermarkt

Noordermarkt

Overlooked by the Noorderkerk, this square has been a market site since 1627. Over the past four centuries it has sold kitchen utensils and *vodden* ('old clothes'), as it still does on Monday mornings. But on Saturdays it becomes the *vogeltjes markt* and sells small birds – chickens, pigeons and budgerigars – from about 6 am to 10 am when it once again transforms itself into a *boerenmarkt*. Like farmers' markets the world over, this fair is a gastronome's dream in terms of healthy, hearty, wholesome organic produce. Popular with locals, it also has appeal for browsers as it exposes the styles and types of food that are popular in the Netherlands. The national obsession with cheese is played out with all the usual suspects (Gouda and Edam), plus varieties of creamy goats and mozzarellas. Bread infused with cheese and baked as a twisty stick is the silencer of choice for mothers with grumpy kids in supermarkets all over Holland, and the organic version here will not disappoint nostalgic fans.

CHILDREN, CHIPS AND CHIC

3 Café-Restaurant Amsterdam

128

4 Restaurant Blue Pepper

Nassaukade 366

The concept behind the name is that blue peppers do not actually exist, an allusion to the culinary dream that Abu Raychanduri is trying to create in his Indonesian restaurant. Indian-born, he grew up in the USA before settling in Amsterdam and engaging the skills of Dutch-born, Indonesian-descended Sonya Henderman, who cooks up the dishes for which this kitchen is fast becoming known: Bebekigall (duck breast served with green sauce), Asinam Segar (fresh mango salad with spicy sour dressing) and, for dessert, the Pisang Blue Pepper (banana with pistachio, peanut, caramel and orange-juice sauce). The result is a food fetishist's fantasy.

IN THE MIX

5 Blender

STREET ART

6 SM Bureau Amsterdam

Rozenstraat 59

Just as New York's MoMA has PS1, so Amsterdam's Stedelijk Museum has its 'street' space with the Bureau. Not surprisingly, the off-shoot gallery is used to profile more experimental work and as such has gained notoriety on the art circuit for the stimulating ideas and statement shows that have been exhibited there. Tucked down a typically quiet Jordaan backstreet, the SM Bureau is hard to find and will appeal to contemporary art fans who enjoy a challenge – both physical and intellectual.

CONTEMPORARY ART ON AN INTERNATIONAL SCALE

7 Torch

Lauriergracht 94

Torch is both loved and hated because of its daring programme. It is the Netherlands's premier gallery for contemporary art and the Dutch name that has consistently appeared on the international art-fair circuit since Adriaan van der Have founded it in 1984 as a podium for young contemporary art. The space is designed by the architect Peter Sas and is located in an area renowned for galleries featuring young artists. Torch itself represents Anton Corbijn, Annie Sprinkle, Ellen Kooi and Teun Hocks and sells the incredible wonderpills (which solve all life's problems) by Dana Wyse. Twenty years of cutting-edge art were celebrated with a commemorative show in 2004.

LIVING 2000 INTERNATIONAL DESIGN CENTRE

8 Wonen / 2000 IDC

Rozengracht 219–23

When Mr Smithuyzen renamed his family business – which has existed in Amsterdam since 1896 – 'Wonen 2000' some 35 years ago, the '2000' had all the connotations of a space odyssey and was the perfect platform for the rising profile of contemporary furniture design. The year may now be out of date but the stores are not. In premises spread over three sites on the busy Rozengracht (two interconnect and the third is across the street) he sells the full house of international design players, but the Edra, Driade and Jacobson ranges are balanced by the presence of Dutch design at its peak. The Gispen discontinued line of steel-tube-framed office furniture, so popular in the 1950s, was revived in 1990 and has been selling here ever since. Artifort are probably the most famous Dutch furniture manufacturers, and their revolving 'Little Tulip' chair is sold in a whole spectrum of colours that includes lime and deep mauve. The 'Lagos' bench is part of the Dutch landscape, as it is used as public seating across the Netherlands. Smithuyzen's team of 20 interior designers man the shops and brasserie that were designed by the local architect legend Cees Nagelkerke.

DESIGN ON TEXTILES

9 DOTShop

Haarlemmerdijk 71

After graduating in fashion design at Amsterdam's fashion academy in 1998, identical twin sisters Mirielle and Marit Platjouw formed a company called Doppia M-Design (Italian for the two initial 'M's of their first names). By 2000 this had evolved into purely textile design, so when they opened their first shop in Amsterdam in 2001, they christened it with their new name. Today the team has grown to include the interior designer Ricky Nypels and Mirielle's husband, Alireza Nikbakht Fini, as marketing strategist. They sell cushions, fabrics and lampshades designed with flockprints, lasercuts and screenprints from three shops in Holland. Their designs are bold, modern and graphic, playful and fun. Strong use of colour and fearless shapes are pointing the way for the DOTShop to join other internationally recognized fabric manufacturers.

GIN DISTILLERY

10   Café 't Smalle

Egelantiersgracht 12

This tiny bar has remained true to its roots as one of the city's oldest brown bars. In 1786 Pieter Hoppe, of Hoppe & Jenever, the first ever distillers of gin, opened it, and the same copper chandelier still hangs over 21st-century moonshine seekers; the cash register bears the date of 1886. The slim space was previously under the ownership of the late legendary Freddy Heineken, who kept this national monument in museum condition. The café must have strange global appeal as the Japanese have built an exact replica of it in their Holland Village in Nagasaki.

SING LIKE A BIRD

11   Finch

149

SMOKIN'

12   Café Tabac

Brouwersgracht 101

Philippe and Georgy Bedier de Prairie own this low-key café as well as Vakzuid (p. 128) and Fishes (p. 89). Their Dutch–Indonesian heritage inspired the dishes, such as Satay Tabac and Chicken Satoagan, which come in generous portions. In keeping with their other establishments, the brothers asked Paul Lindse to design the interior, to evoke travel to the Dutch East Indies.

STANDARD

13   Bordewijk

Noordermarkt 7

Will Demandt opened his first restaurant in 1985, and it has since gained a reputation for honest food inspired by farmers' cooking. Demandt is a self-taught chef and he personally oversees all aspects of running the restaurant. The interior itself is the only remaining example of this type of work by the designer Rob Eckhardt, who has now moved exclusively into furniture design.

BEDOUIN BAZAAR

14   Nomads

150

POPE'S ISLAND

15   Café 't Papeneiland

144

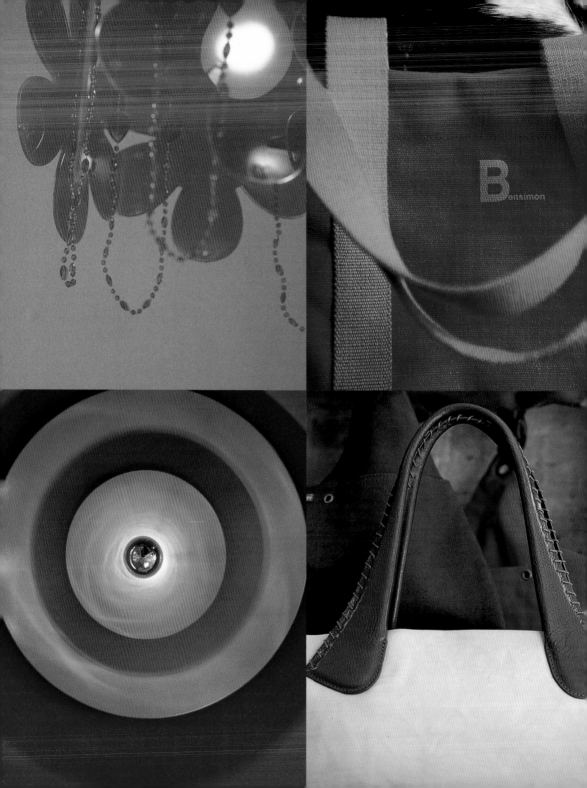

ILLUMINATION ART
16 Voorwerp
Haarlemmerplein 13 hs

Studio Voorwerp is, as its name suggests, a little more personal than your average light shop: it is a made-to-measure illumination design emporium. For more than ten years Voorwerp has designed lamps based on the premise that 'they should be more than functional' and can enhance the aesthetic of the environment they light. Commissions from PTT Telecom (for whom they made promotional gifts in the Netherlands and a three-metre-wide chandelier in Budapest), Sissy Boy Good Morning (clothes retailer), Café de Jaren (p. 134) and the Volta cultural centre in Amsterdam bear testimony to their rising profile as lighting designers. A permanent collection has organically evolved over the past decade and every year two new ones are added. Their use of contrasting and complementary materials has resulted in Candle Lights, patina-coated steel in green and brown that spiral, twisting through the air. Their spindly steel candelabras are reinforced with rubber and contrast with the industrial look of varnished steel, aluminium and sand-blasted glass tubes of their Arosa light.

BAGS OF MONEY
17 Cellarrich
Haarlemmerdijk 98

The four women behind Cellarrich met at teacher training college and still have part-time jobs in education. Sacha Rowald, Miriam Lommers, Minet van Schaik and Ally Liefhebber all shared a love of designing and making leather goods and clothes, so they opened a studio- retail-space in a subterranean shop (the 'cellar' in their name) in the hope that it would bring them fame and fortune ('rich' completing the Cellarrich brand). The dream is coming true, and they now work out of a larger, ground-level store and show annually at the Paris Prêt-à-Porter Première Classe. Each bag and wallet is cut and compounded by the girls so each is individual. Because there are so many people in the production mix, there is choice ranging from clasp-close evening bags in fancy plastics to washable suede or cowhide.

CHECK YOUR OIL
18 Meeuwig & Zn

163

inspiring bread and delicacy

Dimitri and Diante Roels have been baking for six years. Their bread supplies restaurants across the Netherlands, and they finally realized a career-long ambition in 2002 with this, their first shop. The outlet is industrial and contemporary, a clean, white counter divides the space, and there is wall-bar seating, should customers feel like eating their purchases on site. Contemporary graphics and asymmetric display shelving make this a modern bakery like no other. They offer a diverse range of breads from regular whites, browns and wholemeal to lemon, ginger, basil and garlic and even an anchovy variety.

Sander Louwerens's restaurant could easily be mistaken for a stuffy old public house. But anyone put off by the frontage would be missing out on simple, quality cuisine. Louwerens trained in Michelin-star restaurants and uses that experience to enhance his plain honest attitude towards food. He buys in only seasonal fish, meat and game, so choice is dictated by the time of year. While the clientele is often 'rich and famous', the surroundings are comfortably anonymous. Look out for a favourite dessert, 'hang-up': yoghurt strained through a hanging cloth for 24 hours and then mixed with cream and infused with vanilla.

Selling the nation's favourite cakes, sweets and chocolates since 1882, J.G. Beune is a treat for both eyes and stomach. The shop is tiny and oh-so-quaint with an original glass-fronted counter and a resplendent chandelier hanging low over the choice of goodies awaiting packaging in ribbon-wrapped boxes. Butter-cakes, chocolate-piece cakes, *speculaas* (a cinnamon-infused cookie, popular with coffee), cream cakes and apple tarts sit enticingly alongside the other pastries and chocolates that current owners Wim Rombouts and Goos Verboom assure are *hemel op aarde* ('heaven on earth').

Madelon Witterholt makes trips to southern Europe at least once a month, bringing back furniture, pottery, garden hardware and sculpture. Her love of antiques from the area was born from years spent in Italy working as an archaeologist. The pieces that she finds in Spain, France and Italy are distributed over two shops (the other is south of Amsterdam) and are often snapped up by local dealers who know she has a good eye. Although she falls in love with certain objects, Witterholt never keeps anything back, and as the turnover in the shop is always changing, it can look very different even if there are only a few weeks between visits.

Westelijke Grachten
Negen Straatjes
Zuid-Westelijke Grachten

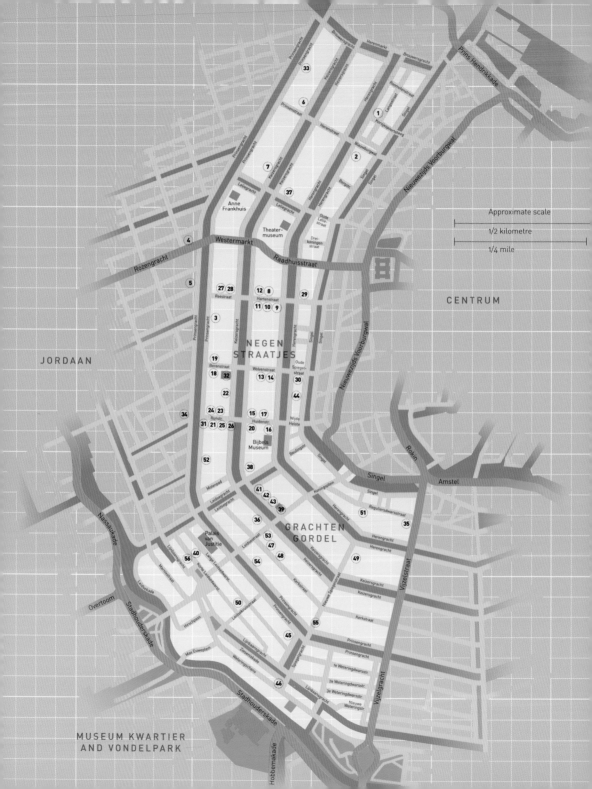

CENTRUM

Approximate scale

1/2 kilometre

1/4 mile

JORDAAN

NEGEN
STRAATJES

GRACHTEN
GORDEL

MUSEUM KWARTIER
AND VONDELPARK

Anne
Frankhuis

Theater-
museum

Westermarkt

Raadhuisstraat

Rozengracht

Palais
van
Justitie

Bijbels
Museum

Prins Hendrikkade

Nieuwezijds Voorburgwal

Nieuwezijds Voorburgwal

Rokin

Amstel

Singel

Singel

Vijzelstraat

Stadhouderskade

Hobbemakade

Nassaukade

Overtoom

33

6

1

2

7

37

4

5

27 28

12 8

29

11 10 9

3

19

18 32

13 14

30

44

22

24 23

34

15 17

31 21 25 26

20

16

52

38

41

42

43 39

51

35

36

53

47

48

49

54

40

56

50

55

45

46

The imposing stone façades and impressive doors around Amsterdam's *grachten gordel* (canal ring) are the most prestigious addresses in the city. Commenced at the beginning of the 17th century, the building of the grand canal rings heralded Amsterdam's Golden Age, when it became the most powerful trading city in the world. Merchant traders built the fashionable houses on four major rings around the Centrum. The Singel was the original medieval moat of the city, and its curving shape is reflected first by the Herengracht ('Gentlemen's Canal', named after the men who invested in it), then by the Keizersgracht (after the Holy Roman Emperor Maximilian I) and finally the Prinsengracht (honouring William, Prince of Oranje). Today, the houses are more likely to be occupied by corporations than individuals.

Some affluent private residences remain, and some, even in their original form, have been gifted to the nation as museums. Those houses that are used as private homes present windows overlooking the canal and are rarely curtained, privacy being an attribute held low on the list of Dutch sensibilities. Passers-by are offered a fantasy-inducing opportunity to view the stylish interiors (mostly kitchens just below street level) of these converted abodes.

Just south of the Raadhuisstraat, the cross-streets that intersect the canals down to the Leidsegracht are known as the *negen straatjes* or 'nine little streets' (the letters 'je' or 'jes' on the end of any Dutch noun denote 'little'). They are rich in café and boutique culture, and some of the most uniquely themed shops of the city await discovery. Interspersed among local specialist bakeries and curiosity shops, the choices featured here are just a selection, so rich is the density of consumer decadence along these *straatjes*.

One of the most delightful elements of walking or biking in Amsterdam is that you will happen across what appear to be hidden backstreets. Their first impression as unassuming alleyways forms an effective filter for the tourist trails, leading the sex-and-drugs seeker away from what is local stomping ground. The Kerkstraat, Reguliersdwarsstraat (or gay street) and alleyways that lead off the neon chaos of the Leidseplein are all home to stylish nightclubs, restaurants and shops that are only distinguishable from their garish neighbours by the style-trained eye, which is all that is needed to tap into the Amsterdam of locals. Design and architecture studios are also frequently located a mere stone's throw from the arterial streets. Knowledge — such as that provided here — is the key to discovering an entirely different side to the city from the stoned misconception that colours its reputation.

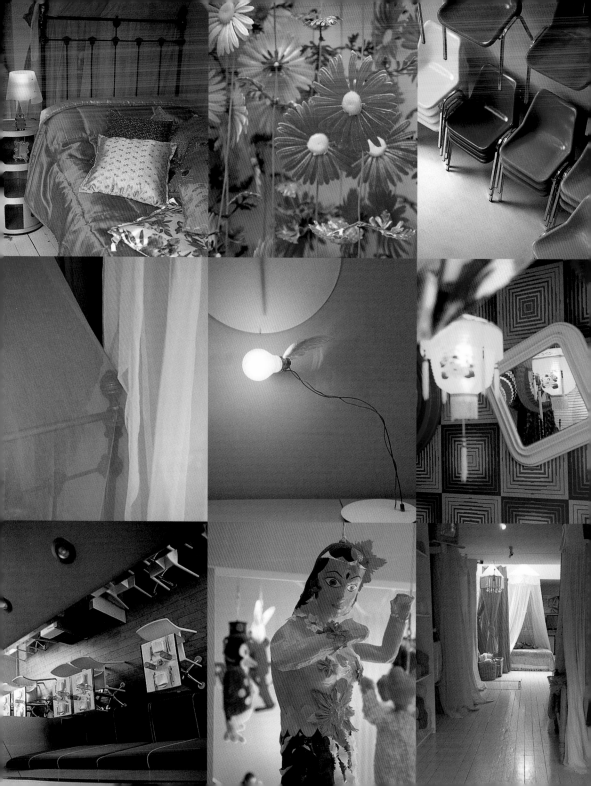

1 Liesbeth Royaards
Herengracht 70b

Dutch women are generally well dressed and veer more towards traditional–professional than experimental styles. Liesbeth Royaards's sense of this has kept her in business for over 35 years. She works out of her studio store at the sober Centraal Station end of the Herengracht, from where she cuts strong suits in wool, silk, linen and cotton, although she says, 'I am interested in new textiles, and see that the sports industry is working with fabrics that react to temperature changes in different ways from the natural fibres, but for now I work with what is around.' Yet that can lead to surprises, not least in the form of the sexy, schoolma'amish, steel-boned corsets that she makes 'to keep clients in'.

2 Sauna Deco
Herengracht 115

Sauna Deco must be experienced by any body-treatment lover. Husband-and-wife team Mr Snabel and Mvr Visser acquired the Dudok-designed building in the 1970s and installed a stunning Art Déco interior from Au Bon Marché in Paris. Guests pay a nominal entrance fee and leave all clothes in the unisex dressing room. Modesty is abandoned at the entrance as you walk around the two saunas, steam room, outside terraces and sculptured plunge pool wrapped only in a towel, which should be left at the door of the treatment rooms and pool. Look out for a large red button at the side of the deep freezing plunge pool; you would be forgiven for thinking it is an alarm call but if you press it the effect is a blast of current-creating water to allow for a proper swim. There are lounge beds for sleeping and all-day massages from several masseurs. This place is a temple to the open, practical, Continental attitude to bare bodies, health and relaxation.

3 TamTam
Prinsengracht 381

The name of this restaurant is appropriated from the first syllable of owner–architect Umit Tambil's surname and the phonetic tom-tom drum coincidence. He and his wife, Ricky, spent 23 years in New York, during which he built an award-winning reputation, participating in architectural projects with retail department stores Barneys, Bloomingdale's and Macy's. Time in the Big Apple is apparent in the inspiration for TamTam. The two-storey-high glass façade is unusual and creates a fantastic contrast on the grand canal. Fusion food is served on the ground floor and there is a champagne bar upstairs.

4 Kitsch Kitchen
Rozengracht 8–12

Spread over two floors, Kitsch Kitchen boasts a colour scheme that is a kaleidoscopic hallucination. It sells a wonderful array of plastic bowls, cups and cutlery and kitchen furniture. There is a vast selection of wallpaper from the 1960s and 1970s, all of which would look perfect on the set of *Abigail's Party*. Such a visually busy store, whose products provide colour and playfulness, stands out in a design world that so often celebrates the idea that 'less is more'. In Kitsch Kitchen, 'more' is definitely more.

5 Klamboe Unlimited
Prinsengracht 232

Edwin van Hellenberg Hubar has been designing *klamboes* (mosquito nets) for more than 20 years. He supplies them in every colour, shape and size for decoration in the home and for their intended function when travelling. Fashions come and go, but he noticed that mosquito nets take on the romantic aspect of a four-poster bed in a northern European home. The shop also sells soft furnishings and little lamps to use when inside the nets.

6 Galerie Binnen
Keizersgracht 82

Helen van Ruiten opened a small interior design studio in the early 1980s. Her business and reputation have grown, and today her space is a well-respected platform for Dutch and international designers selected for the singularity of their design. The gallery is divided between an exhibition area and a retail showroom, which takes popular pieces from the shows and displays them for sale. Among many others, van Ruiten looks after the Dutch designers Maria van Kesteren and Ineke Hans, whose star is in the ascendant in the furniture design arena.

7 Canal House Hotel
114

8 BLGK
Hartenstraat 28

The uniform geometry of the letters is the first indicator of the smart, slick, clean lines that BLGK embodies. The name is composed of the initials of the surnames of the four designers who comprise this jewelry team. Eline Bosma, Marijke te Loo, Wouter de Gruijter and Marit de Koomen all met at the State School of Silver and Goldsmiths, Jewelers and Clockmakers in Schoonhoven in southern Holland in 1978. The town is also known as the 'Silver City' of the Netherlands, and its annual graduates are some of the most sought-after in the industries of traditional craftsmen. Armed with these impeccable credentials, the four friends opened shop in 1995 and, although Bosma is no longer an active member of the crew, BLGK are still making rings, bracelets and necklaces, exquisitely crafted in silver and gold and adorned with precious gems.

9 JOOT

157

10 De Ridder

155

11 Hester van Eeghen
Hartenstraat 37

Van Eeghen has operated her production of colourful leather goods from this shop since 1988. The popularity of her bags, wallets, purses and, most recently, shoes, has resulted in her supplying over 100 outlets across the Netherlands, Germany, Switzerland and Japan. Her designs are eye-catching, both because of their bright colours (she uses vibrant reds and acid limes as well as more neutral shades of leather) and their bold shapes, which appear inspired by architecture and sculpture. As such, the work is frequently featured in museum shows (the Stedelijk, Amsterdam), and she has taken part in a charity auction at Sotheby's, where she sold over 20 unique pieces. Van Eeghen's status in the leather design industry now means that she is in a position to help promote newer young designers, and she actively conceives projects and competitions that run through the academies in the Netherlands.

12 Analik
161

13 Wolvenstraat 23
Wolvenstraat 23

People refer to this eaterie as '23' or 'Wolvenstraat' or 'the place with no name', as the owners Rob Benoni, Anna Mol and Laurens Stegge decided not to christen it in the usual way. The anonymity has worked to its advantage, automatically providing first-time customers with a feeling that they have found something off the beaten track. Benoni met Mol when she worked for him at Finch (p. 149), the bar he owns in the Jordaan, and in 1999 they teamed up with *horeca* financial powerhouse Stegge, who also has Bond and the Chocolate Bar in his evolving empire. With Arne Oosterbaan's expertise they created a 1970s-style lounge, with shag-pile carpet leading up the stairs to the loos and some rather lime banquettes. Food is great here because Asian-inspired noodle soup, jellyfish or oysters all feature on one menu alongside quality sandwiches and Euro-breakfasts. Finally, not eating the Chinese option does not mean being stuck with 'egg and chips'.

14 H.J. van de Kerkhof
Wolvenstraat 9–11

A third generation of Kerkhofs are currently the proud caretakers of the family business that was conceived by Grandfather Kerkhof in 1939. Although his professional talents extended to interior design, during the bombing raids of the Second World War the skills of a curtain hanger with heavy black-out drapes were in demand and the store was kept busy for its first few years of existence. For many years it has sold an assortment of braids, tassels and adornments, which cover the walls of the haberdashery. To enter is to walk into a sewing box; buttons, ribbons, pins, tape, wool and fabrics spill from their reels and cases. The tactile equivalent of finger food overcomes discipline, and it is impossible to resist stroking or brushing the velvets, cottons and rope twists that fill the little space. As you would expect, Kerkhof's clients include fashion designers and students, haberdashery-happy-hobbyists and people looking for that odd button.

15 Christian Best

Keizersgracht 357

'Jan Best' is the name on the window of the lamp shop that has been here for over 40 years. The store occupies a corner space and is full of lights, hanging and standing and perching on surfaces. The family business was passed from father to son and today is managed by Christian. His time is spent travelling all over Europe, looking for lamps at auctions and antique markets. Their reputation means that he is frequently the first port of call for people who inherit or want to sell old lamps. He has sold chandeliers from Russian palaces and been invited to oversee the sale of lamps from old castles. Best also designs his own. He is particularly proud of a tiny desk lamp that is reminiscent of a white foxglove hanging tentatively from a drooping brass stalk.

AN ELEPHANT'S FANTASY

16 Ozenfant

Huidenstraat 3–5

The name is a childish corruption of the word elephant, according to the owner–designer Faas van Dijk, who is responsible for the 50 or so pieces of abstract-inspired furniture. Handmade in Holland, the sofas, tables and chairs are displayed in his low-key premises. Ozenfant is only open on Saturdays or by appointment and, as such, Van Dijk's space maintains a studio feel about it that makes ordering pieces from him a very personal experience. There is no sense of ego in the place, and somehow the designer melts into the stone-coloured walls as the eye is drawn to the calmly crafted pieces of furniture.

POMP AND SPLENDOUR

17 Pompadour

132

What appears to be a gallery space featuring art, magazines and books is actually just the public face for creative advertising agency Mendo. The brainchild of Joost Albronda ('Body that can't be copied' is one of three slogans printed on his business card), Ramon Otting ('Boots made for walking' refer to the fact that he rarely changes his footwear) and Roy Rietstap ('Big ears listen'), Mendo was behind campaigns for the Dutch Labour party, UMRO and Fisherman's Friend. 'Mendo' satisfies the healthy egos of these three chaps by encompassing all their projects under one banner. They use the gallery for exhibitions giving the public access to Dutch artists (including their own work), as well as for selling international design literature. The selection of books and magazines is at any time reflective of the changing face of branding, media and graphic representation.

Until recently in the Netherlands, certain academic curricula set exams for people who wanted to work in or run shops. Bernadette de Haan was schooled under this scheme and Parisienne is the result of her endeavours. A frilly, girly, frou-frou jewelry box of a shop (it is only 12 metres square), De Haan has plastered the walls with Victorian boudoir flower-sprouting wallpaper, which adds to its intimate atmosphere. She sells trinkets, necklaces, bracelets, anklets and rings. With pashminas, bags, belts, and shoes, it is a very pretty little place containing plenty of eye-candy for grown-up girls.

Tesser
NIJMEGEN

VENETIAN
BLINDS

2000

nieuw

- Puur Chocola
- Cooking the Roman
- Pesto & Tapenade
- Gary Rhodes: Voorg
                    en Zome
- Pizza
- Only the best: M.Ro

De Kaaskamer

KOH-I-NOOR 701 grote kop	KOH-I-NOOR 702 grote kop	KOH-I-NOOR 794 compacte kop	KOH-I-NOOR 727 grote kop	KOH-I-NOOR 723 grote kop	KOH-I-NOOR 771 extra grote kop

21 Skins
Runstraat 9

Philip Hillege used to work for Herôme, one of the Netherlands's most generic hand- and nail-care companies, when his old business school pal Michael Poelmans approached him to set up a more exclusive outlet for beauty products. Poelmans runs the successful French restaurant JeanJean (which scored a rating of '9' from food journalist Johannes van Dam) with his brother. Skins is unique in the Netherlands for selling niche brand skin- and hair-care lines, such as Aveda, Nuxe, Philosophy and Aesop. The fragrance range includes Creed, Agent Provocateur, Acqua di Genova, candles and room-spray by Diptyque. The shop is conceived as a playground for beauty fanatics who can spray, smear and smell to their noses' content. Skins breaks prudent Dutch protocol by giving away samples and encouraging testing. There is a salon offering treatments and make-overs at the rear of the store where glass windows overlook a decked terrace for clients to sip wine or water, while waiting for their 'frosting' to set.

THE OLD ALMSHOUSE
22 Blakes

120

BOOKS FOR COOKS
23 De Kookboekhandel
Runstraat 26

Whatever tickles your culinary fancy, this store will have a recipe for it. In terms of space and towers of books piled on shelves, it is the chef's equivalent of a dusty magic shop. Second-hand, new, Dutch, English, French, other languages, it seems that every cookbook ever published is in, or has passed through, this tiny smoky space. At any time there is a blackboard on the wall with the current favourites and best-sellers scratched out in chalk. The shop was opened over 20 years ago by the wife of the architect Alexander Bodon. She passed it on to Johannes van Dam, who is now the Netherlands's premier restaurant critic writing in Amsterdam's lefty newspaper *Het Parool* (a '9' will make you, a '6' will break you). He in turn handed it to the current keeper, Jonah Freud, in 1990. She is a also a food journalist, writing for *Elle* and other Dutch press, and recently brought out a Kookboekhandel book for aspiring chefs aged 12–20. The shop remains the first and last word in food.

ASK JEEVES
24 Butler's
Runstraat 22

Marcel Wiggert Hukom's flair for fabulousness means that he has created a designer den in an appropriately design-conscious neighbourhood. Hukom's shop opened only in 2002, but he had been selling Missoni towels and Calvin Klein underwear under the 'Room Service' banner (a similar shop on chi-chi Cornelis Schuytstraat) for the previous 12 years. Butler's is his own endeavour and he has dropped his Calvins for the Dutch underwear brand Claesen. There is also linen for the table, bath and bedroom, some supplied by the Dutch manufacturer HNL. The rest of the store, which has the decadent tones of a masculine boudoir, is an amalgamation of Hukom's hand-picked choice of high-quality aspirational 'must-haves'.

CHEESE
25 De Kaaskamer
Runstraat 7

Edam, Gouda, Leerdamer, mozzarella, cheddar, Montgomery, 'the cheese room' stocks over 300 varieties of cheeses from all over the world. Yet the Dutch are a fiercely proud nation of cheese makers. The local makes dominate the store and are presented as wax-coated solid wheels. This layer means they are durable (although it would be a rare tourist who bought a whole cheese) and will last for some months. Most locals will buy cheese by weight and assistants are on hand to cut specific amounts, so everything can be tasted, savoured and smelled.

THE WHITE TEETH SHOP
26 De Witte Tandenwinkel
Runstraat 5

Sometimes the simplest ideas are the most successful and De Witte Tandenwinkel is just such an idea. Bert Quist has been selling oral-care products from this tiny store since 1980. It is a medicine chest for teeth and its clean, white interior is vaguely reminiscent of a dentist's waiting room. But similarity ends there, as this shop is fun and filled with tooth tools, the likes of which you have never seen before. Floss, picks, brushes, gum and pastes in myriad flavours fill the interior and Quist's favourite brushes hang in the window. Local legend has it that the Rolling Stones wanted to explore the shop, but their faint-hearted security guards would not permit them as the shop has no back escape route.

27 Cortina Papier
Reestraat 22

Once a designer of photo albums, Mieke van den Berg started to sell paper products from her little shop in 1995. Mezzanine tiers divide the space into three levels. Upstairs are photo albums and stationery, on the ground floor notebooks and greeting cards, and below, sheets of wrapping paper. There is a large selection of both journals for diary writing and the student organizers/planners known here as *agendas*. These mid-year bound books appear on the shelves of stationers across the country every summer. The designs encompass TV-cartoon characters, fashion designers or sports labels, and are spot-on indicators of youth-culture obsessions for any given year. Prices vary widely, making the *agenda* a status symbol in certain educational environments. Van den Berg also sells paper from the only functioning paper windmill in the world. Zaandam *molen* (mill) paper is quite rough and thick and its cotton base dictates its final hue (denim makes blue paper). If there is no wind, which is rare in Holland, there will be no paper.

28 What's Cooking
Reestraat 16

This innovative store screams 'stylist' the moment you walk in, and indeed, the owner Jacqueline Overtoom was first a fashion then a retail stylist working for eye-candy magazines such as *Cosmopolitan, Yes* and *Top Santé*. It was a one-off job as a buyer of culinary pieces that first drew her attention to the diversity and choice of bowls, cups and unusual food products, and this led her to see an opening for a shop selling alternative dinner-party gifts. 'Everyone takes a bottle of wine or flowers,' she noted, and so stocked her shop with oils in keepsake bottles, coffees, peppers and fortune cookies. The space incorporates a cavernous basement decorated in magenta, crimson and burnt-ochre, and an upstairs, where the cool hues of indigo, sapphire and emerald complement the natural glint of steel and unvarnished wood.

29 Antonia by Yvette
Gasthuismolensteeg 18–20

Yvette is a rosy-cheeked girl with a love for shoes. Her passion was so great that it spilled out over three adjacent shops (one for women, one for men and one for kids and sporty shoes), and she now houses her changing collections in a larger corner store on the same street. She sells her own line under the name of Antonia, which just happened to be a name she liked. Yvette combines her sexy boots with a stunning selection from other international shoe designers. She really knows her designers – and customers – and the shop is full of desirable footwear from Audley (London designers making elegant, classy models), Hugo Boss (practical, quality), Botticelli (sophisticated bloke), Fly London (comfy boots), Muxart (high, pointy–strappy), Roberto Rinaldi (amazing pointed men's boots) and Sonia Rykiel (dangerous spikes). This is one of those great Amsterdam outlets where the groundwork for picking out the season's choicest shoes and designers is already done.

30 Buffet van Odette & Yvette
Herengracht 309

Odette Rigterink was running a tiny take-out-only *broodje bar* (sandwich shop) across the canal on the Berenstraat when her popularity overtook her capacity to supply the local demand. So she secured a marginally larger outlet and teamed up with Yvette van Vliet. They offer a delicious range of organic food all bought from the Lindenhoff farm. Their fish, meat and poultry come from Frank's Fine Foods and bread is by the neighbourhood's most savoured traditional bakery, Hartog. Their favourite dish: truffle cheese omelette that melts on the tongue.

31 Lust
Runstraat 13

Danny Muller already held a place in the heart of the nation as a football player for Ajax and Barcelona before he decided to take care of the nation's hearts by opening a health-conscious eaterie. 'Travelling all the time with the soccer made me aware how hard it can be to get quality organic fare and trust what you are eating,' he commented. Restaurant critic Johannes van Dam agreed with his sentiments entirely and awarded him a top-class 9 out of 10. Muller's menu includes the de rigueur selection of shakes, salads, sandwiches and juices but also hides some delightful Dutch delicacies in the form of *osseworst*, a sausage typical only of Amsterdam from the acclaimed butcher Hergo. It is best accompanied by pickles from the famous Jewish manufacturer De Leuw and a sharp carrot sauce, *mieret wortel*.

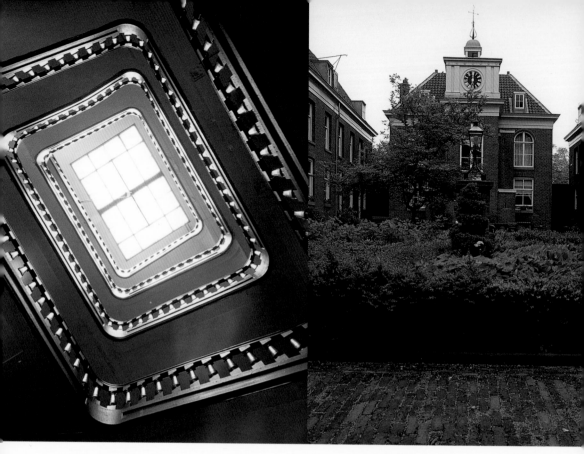

FOR THE PEOPLE
32 Felix Meritis
Keizersgracht 324

'Happiness Through Achievement' is the epigraph carved above the entrance of the Felix Meritis building, which was born as the home of a society of arts and sciences in 1778. The monolithic structure contained a library, observatory, laboratories and a concert hall, and the Felix Meritis Foundation was the cultural centre for the Dutch Enlightenment. But with changing politics and funding it later became the Communist Party headquarters. Today it has been revived as the European Centre for Art and Science and is used for Amsterdam's Summer University. An evolving programme of lectures, courses and discussion groups takes place here, and the institution also stages theatre and dance performances. A café can be found on the ground floor.

SECRET GARDEN
33 Hofje van Brienen
Prinsengracht 89–133

The overcrowded architecture of the older parts of the city (the Jordaan and Centrum) is occasionally broken by a *hofje*. Financed by wealthy merchants in the 17th and 18th centuries, Protestant organizations built hundreds of almshouses around courtyards in which to house the poor and elderly. Visitors to the sanctuary of the courtyards must respect that today they are often privately owned, but some still serve their original purpose (the Begijnhof at Spui [p. 17] being the most famous example). Jan van Brienen founded this *hofje* on the site of the Star Brewery in 1804, and it is colloquially known as the Star Hofje. The story goes that van Brienen was accidentally locked in a vault and was so overjoyed when released that he realized his gratitude in this charitable form. The courtyard is lush and manicured and a visually pleasing contrast to the bricks and mortar that dominate the area.

SOAP

34 La Savonnerie

Prinsengracht 294

ALL ABOUT SHIRTS

35 The Shirt Shop

Reguliersdwarsstraat 64

The Norwegian Turid Nisen has been living in Amsterdam for more than 20 years. She hand-makes all the soaps herself in the shop by a traditional French method, altered to suit her own style. 'I think soap-making is like cooking and every day I arrive and my mood dictates the soap I produce,' she enthuses. The choice spans a wide range – covering all eventualities – with over 80 different scents: jasmine, magnolia, camomile, cut grass and avocado (newer experiments), pine tree and patchouli (old-fashioned scents). Turid has also concocted famous perfume brand scents that are indistinguishable from the real thing, though 'for legal reasons I have to give them different names'. The soaps come in every colour of the spectrum except black.

Located on Amsterdam's 'gay street', this is the peacock of shirt shops. One rail proudly displays almost 100 shirts, each different, each fabulous. The shop is 'product, not label led', as the owners travel across Europe seeking out the trendiest and best quality items, unavailable in Holland, which are then sold exclusively from their shop. There is choice for the more conservative dresser, though The Shirt Shop is a celebration of masculine style. Its predominant range 'aimed at 16- to 60-year-olds' is of slim-cut pieces decorated with colour, cotton and contrast. Up a little staircase, in the upstairs window, are more rails featuring a veritable rainbow of long- and short-sleeved shirts. In keeping with their unusual approach, the shop opens only from 1 pm to 7 pm.

CALVINIST KIMONOS

36 Collette van Landuijt

Keizersgracht 476

Van Landuijt was born in Ghent, Belgium, in 1945 and has been designing clothes in Amsterdam since 1975. The timeless garments are crafted from natural fibres, wool, linen, silk and cotton, as well as viscose and rayon. Although she now has a support team, van Landuijt prefers to work alone, in silence, in her subterranean studio-cum-store, consumed by the privacy of her activity. Her clothes reflect this discipline. They are not trendy: instead they follow the lines of the body, in an erotic yet honourable form. Her plain-coloured textiles allow for draping and wrapping and the versatility of her shapes makes her popular with dancers and actors, whose jobs reject the constriction of more formal traditional tailoring.

HAUTE CUISINE

37 Christophe

PHOTOGRAPHY

38 Huis Marseille

Keizersgracht 401

This gallery is the pre-eminent photography space in Amsterdam. Located in an equally impressive 17th-century house, Huis Marseille (named after the French merchant who built it) is a photography foundation exhibiting Dutch and foreign work. It was inaugurated as the seat of the Foundation for Photography in 1999 after the architects Laurens Vis and Banthem Crouwel adapted the building to host exhibitions by the likes of Daan van Golden and Albert Londe. The regular, curated exhibitions and retrospectives represent both documentary and art and science perspective photography. One recent example was a Wim and Donata Wenders show of pictures that took as its theme the Buena Vista Social Club. Huis Marseille has its own permanent collection of contemporary photography in-house.

DEPARTMENT STORE

39 Metz & Co

Leidsestraat 34–36

This was once the site of Van Gogh's uncle's art shop, but it is now the Netherlands's answer to London's Harrods. In fact, Liberty of London bought it in 1973 and commissioned Cees Dam to design the café on the sixth floor. When it was built in 1891, it was the tallest commercial structure in the city (until very recently, few buildings competed with the churches), designed by the architect Jan van Looy for the New York Life Insurance Company, whose name is still inscribed above the ground-level door. Metz & Co moved there in 1908. Generic contemporary designer fashion and furniture labels are juxtaposed in the settings, which remain old-fashioned with a slight air of pomposity. However, it is worth climbing several flights of stairs to the top floor just to see the café. From this vantage point a rare view over Amsterdam's rooftops can be enjoyed through Rietveld-designed cupola windows.

MOULIN ILLUSION

40 Joia

WHY DON'T YOU?

41 Young Designers United

DRINKING AND ARCHITECTURE

42 Walem

OLD BUT NEW

43 Morlang

142

SAIL AWAY

44 Koan Float

Herengracht 321

Koan Float provides respite in a busy city by offering sessions in 35.5° Celsius, salted water flotation tanks followed by a massage. The flotation tanks are fitted with water filtration systems that provide purified water for each user. Soundproofed fibreglass tanks are equipped with an intercom system, optional ambient stereo and light switches so that the flotation experience meets the needs of each individual. Research shows floating to be an effective remedy for stress and jet lag, as well as an aid for rheumatic pains, reducing blood pressure and fortifying the immune system. Whether fact or fiction, going wrinkly in a tank is not an unpleasant way to spend an afternoon.

45 TinkerBell
Spiegelgracht 10–12

Wooden-toy toyshops in the Netherlands do not have quite the same cult status as they do in English-speaking countries, because they are pretty much the norm. But the toys are still sold as much to adults for interior decoration as they are for kids' use. Gerrit Braaksma's homey old shop was already an established toy emporium when he acquired it in 2001; in fact, he had been working there himself for the previous seven years. The first breath of nostalgia comes in the shape of an enormous cabinet full of *knickers* ('marbles', and pronounced 'k-nickers'). There are traditional tin toys and wooden crafted rocking horses and doll's houses, as well as a delightful range of pine and beech toddler toys that double so well as ornaments.

46 Reflex Modern Art Gallery
Weteringschans 79

The Reflex is an active player on the CoBrA art stage. Karel Appel's and Theo Wolvecamp's work is channelled through the gallery, along with pieces from the 1960s Fluxus movement and New Realism period. In 1997 Reflex Art started its miniature museum project with work by over 500 artists. The condition for inclusion was that the work be small, and this endeavour found them a place in the Guinness Book of Records. The collection includes over 1,500 pieces by Annie Liebowitz, Yves Klein, Joseph Beuys, Sol LeWitt and Dutch artists Jan Cremer, Rob Scholte, Anton Rooshens and Marte Roling. Ironically, its size meant they had to move it to another venue.

47 Lambiek
Kerkstraat 119

Kees Kousemaker opened Europe's first antiquarian comic store in 1968. Over 30 years later, Lambiek is famous for a vast collection of rare and obscure comics from all over the world. Comic collecting is a national pastime and Lambiek's clientele extends well beyond young boys spending pocket money. The store is named after an amiable character from the comic strip *Suske & Wiske* by the Dutchman Willy Vandersteen, and also as a pun on 1960s store names, which often ended in 'iek'. Fans of cartoon art will be excited by the selection here.

48 De Witte Voet
Kerkstraat 135

Annemie Boissevain has owned a gallery since 1975. She noticed that artists were using ceramics to create non-functional objects and her shows tend to highlight the potential of clay as more than just crockery. In 1987 Boissevain joined forces with Galerie Ra and the Crafts Council (UK) to present 'New Art Objects' by Dutch and British artists. She currently looks after the ceramicists Rod Bugg, Piet Stockmans, Elly de Goede and Tejo Philips.

49 Pygma-Lion
129

50 De Blonde Hollander
131

51 Bar ARC
147

52 The Frozen Fountain
156

53 Paul Warmer
160

54 Seven One Seven
106

55 Spiegelkwartier

- Eduard Kramer, Nieuwe Spiegelstraat 64
- Dekker Antiquairs, Spiegelgracht 9

For centuries, Amsterdam has counted among the major antique centres of Europe. The Rokin and surrounding areas have the oldest reputation in this collector arena. But since the construction of the Rijksmuseum at the turn of the 19th century, the Spiegelstraat, which runs down to its architectural entrance from the city centre, evolved as the 'new' antique neighbourhood. The antiquarians who set up shop offer an impressive selection of antique art, paintings, ceramics, glass, coins, jewelry, books, furniture and of course Delft Blue tiles. The range and knowledge of the staff at Kramer is unsurpassed, and entrance into this family business requires delicate manoeuvring around cabinets, ornaments and precariously placed pieces. Dekker Antiquairs's collection of Jacobean twist glassware belongs in a museum, as do the finds in many of the shops that line this stretch. Unless you are a serious collector, the shops are best enjoyed as an art and history lesson, and chatting to dealers is usually rewarding; with their experience and knowledge they could be running departments in art institutions.

WHO'S THAT GUY?
56 Jimmy Woo
Korte Leidsedwarsstraat 16–18

Some 15 years ago, Amsterdam's nightclubbing art world was going crazy for Seymour Likely, whose club was all the rage on the Nieuwezijds Voorburgwal. But Mr Likely was actually the mythical embodiment of several local artists who created him as a spin exercise. So too is Jimmy Woo. His club is really the latest project for Casper Reijnders (Joia [p. 148]), who has once again employed the talents of B. Inc Interior Stuff to create a Studio 54-cum-Shanghai-glamorama as the plaything of Triad Tycoon Mr Woo. B. Inc's Eric Kuster has switched on thousands of light bulbs over the 100-square-metre dance floor and dabbled with a palette of gold, magenta and black. Softer shadows cascade from huge Chinese lanterns onto the antique divans. The eclectic club opened at the end of 2003 and is pulling in an eccentric mix of local hipsters and sophisticrats. On the opening night, the tattoo artist Henk Schiffmacher drew tattoos in invisible ink on to the limbs of willing volunteers, whose guinea-pig role guarantees them permanent free club access. The whole show is overseen from the VIP room, where Mr Woo is always rumoured 'to be coming later'.

Museum Kwartier
Vondelpark

Located at the south-eastern corner of the Vondelpark, the Museum Kwartier is a phenomenon of ongoing town planning that can finally be called a success. This part of the city was farmland right up to the end of the 1800s, when the city council decided to improve it and designated it an area of art and cultural enlightenment in Amsterdam. They constructed the world-famous Rijksmuseum, which is home to many familiar faces of the Dutch masters (Rembrandt's *The Night Watch* or *The Company of Captain Frans Banning Cocq*, and Vermeer's *The Milkmaid*), and followed this success with what has become the city's pioneer of modern art, the Stedelijk Museum (p. 72) and the unrivalled acoustics of the Concertgebouw. The Van Gogh Museum opened in 1973 and development continues with its latest extension (p. 72), completed in 1999, and the addition of a huge lawn, pond and urban skate park on the Museumplein, which forms the somewhat barren landscape between these venerable art institutions. The square itself is still used as a site for political demonstrations.

Just to the west of this green patch lies Amsterdam's back garden. The Vondelpark was named after the Dutch poet and playwright Joost van den Vondel in 1867 and his statue stands in the 44 hectares (110 acres) of grass, trees and pastures that are home to ducks, squirrels, cows, goats, llamas and a flock of parakeets, whose daily feeding in front of the pavilion is a spectacle in its own right. Every week the park becomes the meeting point for the Friday Night Skate, when hundreds of rollerbladers convene and take over the cycle paths. J.D. and L.P. Zocher were the father and son landscape architects (commissioned in 1864) responsible for laying this land, mirroring English parks with their winding paths, ponds and lakes to create an illusion of space in the inner city. The park also holds a cultural role with the presence nearby of the Nederlands Filmmuseum and the neoclassical building of De Hollandsche Manege riding school (p. 72).

The streets surrounding the park are naturally where the Amsterdam elite live, their proximity to the green space ensuring astronomic house prices. The designer-brand-clad P.C. Hooftstraat is testimony to the Dutch love for labels. Further west the Cornelis Schuytstraat plays the affluent local high street perfectly, with boutiques selling a hand-picked choice of catwalk fashion, delicatessens replacing the ubiquitous Albert Heijn grocery stores and two of Amsterdam's finest florists, Menno Kroon (p. 158) and Thera de Groot.

The restaurants and hotels in this part of town further reflect the cash-rich clientele for whom they cater. It's certainly swanky but the Dutch low-key tone prevents the usual intimidation factor from being added to the mix.

This is the home of one of the largest modern art collections in the Netherlands. It is revered for its De Stijl collection with work by Piet Mondrian and Theo van Doesburg. It was also the first to host a CoBrA show in 1949. Not all the works can be displayed simultaneously because of the sheer number. Today, the permanent collection is presented alongside temporary exhibitions by Inez van Lamsweerde, Cindy Sherman and Marina Abramovic, to name but a few.

The main structure of this museum, which houses the world's largest collection of Dutch masters, was designed by the renowned Dutch architect Gerrit Rietveld and opened in 1973. Rietveld actually died in 1964, but his drawings were used to complete the building. A new wing was added to the museum in 1999 for which the commission was won by the Japanese architect Kisho Kurokawa, whose international repertoire already included museums in Japan and the airport at Kuala Lumpur. His work sits well beside the black lines and geometric shapes that characterize Rietveld's design; the cones, ellipses and squares form a symbiosis between Western rational geometry and Eastern asymmetry.

Where do you go to get a cosmopolitan with essence of orange blasted inside the martini glass? To find garden solace in the middle of a bustling city? To sleep in rooms where youngsters once studied? The College Hotel is set to be Amsterdam's answer to service and style on the international playing field. And playing field is no pun, as this hotel is opening up in a former school. Wide banistered staircases, 5-metre-high ceilings, raw brick and an enormous gymnasium – transformed into a gourmet dining extravaganza – are testimony to the former role of this 1895 building. A new lease of life is provided by Amsterdam's Hotel School, who chose Stijlnet (concepts) and FG Stijl Architecture & Interior Design to realize their 'old school' fantasy. The chairman of the Amsterdam Hotel Association instigated the project, concerned that the craft of service was being diluted by the onslaught of bright, bold, designer hotels. Indeed, the charm of The College Hotel is enhanced when you realize it is staffed by a new generation of hotel employees about to graduate. A fact you'd never know unless told.

The façade of De Hollandsche Manege, built in 1882, provides a grand entrance to the national riding school, although access to it is via a nondescript entrance on the Vondelstraat. A.L. van Gendt (who was also responsible for the nearby Concertgebouw) based his design on the Spanish Riding School in Vienna. Public outrage saved it from demolition in the 1980s, and it was reopened by Prince Bernhard in 1986, having been restored to its original grandeur. From a balcony café (which serves typically Dutch snacks, such as chips with mayonnaise and croquettes), visitors can witness dressage classes and show-jumping practice in the sawdust arena. The neoclassical interior is a reminder of the importance that high society once accorded good horsemanship.

WITTE WIJNEN   **BOND**

Doornbos, South Africa (per glas 3)

2001 Montravel, Domaine du Gouyat (per glas 3.3)
Fris, uitbundig, mooie zuren en nobele moufvullend.

2002 Touraine, Sauvignon Blanc, Domaine de l'Aumonier
2001 Picpoul de Pinet, Felines Jourdan, Languedoc
Druitig en perfecte visbegeleider (en schelp- en schaaldieren).

2000 Vernaccia della Luna, Toscana
Elegant met ingetogen indrukken van bloemen, citroenmelisse en amandel.

2001 Pinot Bianco, Alois Lageder Pinot Blanc uit Noordoost Italië.
Gerotelde berglucht uit Alto Adige

2001 Domaine Millet Frères Sancerre Blanc
Fris fruitige, tikje kruidige en elegante wijn.

2001 Serge Dagueneau, Pouilly Fumé
Frisse appels en zuidvruchten, sappige zuren.

1999 Sybille Kuntz Riesling &
Heerlijk open, citrus

11 Cobra

Hobbemastraat 18, Museumplein

Sitting in the middle of the huge grass *plein* (square) that joins the 'big three' Amsterdam museums (the Rijksmuseum, the Stedelijk and the Van Gogh) is a café inspired by the CoBrA art movement. 'CoBrA' stands for Copenhagen, Brussels and Amsterdam, the cities where the member artists lived. The café is to CoBrA what Disneyland is to Mickey and Minnie, but it does provide a swift taste of the main players alongside a coffee and *appeltaart*. The building was by Spanjers; a Eugène Brands painting inspired the design of the flooring and chairs; Theo Wolvekamp was used for the staff aprons; Shinkichi Tajiri designed the trellis on the upper deck; and a bronze Karel Appel statue oversees the circus. The grass-covered Museumplein is an equally popular meeting place and was the work of the Danish landscape architect Sven-Ingvar Andersson. An impressive view of the Rijksmuseum can be had from a triangular grass verge that rises into the sky to form the roof of an Albert Heijn store (the most familiar supermarket in the country).

12 Bond

Valeriusstraat 128-B

The wide, tree-lined streets around the Vondelpark shelter an affluent residential neighbourhood of Amsterdam, and the shops, bars and restaurants (Bond included) reflect this. Ed van Zomeren opened the bar in 2002 with Nicole Disdergen and Laurens Stegge. They also own the 1970s-style Chocolate Bar in De Pijp and Stegge adds Wolvenstraat 23 (p. 52) to his personal triune. They named this bar as a 'corny dig at the pomp and splendour of the area', explains van Zomeren, but he also intended the interior style to appeal to the chic locals. With top-notch credentials in the *horeca* industry earned at Seymour Likely (in the club's heyday in the 1990s) and Finch (p. 149), van Zomeren's foray into design was instinctive: the 'Bond world' in his mind has been realized with the plushness of a 1950s hotel lobby.

13 't Blauwe Theehuis

Vondelpark 5

The Baanders brothers were architects of the Nieuwe Zakelijkheid school and built 't Blauwe Theehuis in 1928 to resemble a flying saucer just landed in the Vondelpark.

The building is so unusual – round tiers rise up like a pale wedding cake, the structure secured with spindle poles – that it was declared a listed building, but the Monumentenzorg (overseers of monuments or listed buildings) have permitted its use as a café-bar. It has the largest terrace in Holland (seating 700) and plays classic movies upstairs in the winter.

14 Le Garage & En Pluche

- Ruysdaelstraat 54–56
- Ruysdaelstraat 48

What is the speed of gossip? Just slower than the speed of light at Le Garage, where whispers and glances bounce off more mirrors than a disco ball. Celebrities and those who want to see/be them flock to Joop Braakhekke's sister eateries (Le Garage and En Pluche are located next door to one another in this swanky neighbourhood) like moths to a flame. And combustion is often the conclusion of an evening as, 'who is dining with whom and who said what to whom' is the menu of choice at both establishments, the salacious appetite filler for a 'carte' that lists French cuisine at Le Garage and tapas-style titbits at En Pluche. Braakhekke is no stranger to fame himself and is as familiar to the nation as the 'soapies' (as the Dutch refer to their beloved soap-opera starlets) that frequent his establishments, via his own schedule of television cooking appearances. Happily, the food does not suffer for his absence from the kitchen.

15 Blaine's B&B at the Park

112

16 Aziz

Overtoom 259

Without any formal training, Aziz began designing wedding dresses 27 years ago. Since then, he has built a nationwide reputation on the backs of Holland's most elite brides. He prefers to design dresses for women over 30, believing that they have the emotional maturity he demands from the wearers of his couture. He sees the making of the dresses as a process where he and the client put in enough time for him to understand her wedding dream, which he attempts to realize in a gown that will walk her down the aisle. More recently, Aziz has been working on a range of wedding bedding and has opened a unique bed and breakfast called Suite 259 above his atelier.

17 Fred de la Bretonière
Van Baerlestraat 34

This is a household name for shoes in Holland and it is surprising that Fred's talents have not pushed him further into international footwear. He was born in 1944 and opened his first shop in Amsterdam in 1970, from where he sold shoes, belts and rough leather accessories. His lack of formal training meant that he accidentally applied nonconformist methods to his work: 'For example, I bought my iron clasps at the iron shop instead of the haberdashery and that was hot and new,' he explained. His first shoes were wooden soled, and he would fit leather directly around a client's foot. By 1976 his innovation was recognized with the 'Best shoe-and-bag designer in the Netherlands' award. Today his work is available through seven of his own shops and many other outlets; he also designs ranges for several of the main Dutch labels such as Turnover and Van Dalen.

FISH FOOD

18 Brasserie Bark
Van Baerlestraat 120

This building was home to a quality butcher for more than a century before the owners decided to reinvent it as a fish restaurant over ten years ago. Hans Janssen was already a butcher by trade when he asked Marja (whose father owned the butcher building) to marry him. They wed and he started working in the new 'family business'. But the central location of the site and its proximity to the culture honey pots of the Concertgebouw and museums called for a change that came about in the form of Bark. They keep the kitchen open late and take full advantage of exceptional sealife brought in daily by Dutch and Belgian fisherfolk – crustaceans, shellfish, lobster, scallops, fresh North Sea crab and a variety of oysters: creuses, fines de Claires, Marennes and Belons. Fish choices include salmon, Dover sole, swordfish and tuna. Like the menu, the interior is busy and the colour scheme a little hectic.

MADE-TO-MEASURE

19 Possen.com
161

ELIXIR OF LIFE

20 De Waterwinkel
165

BOOKS ABOUT ART

21 ArtBook

Van Baerlestraat 126

The proximity of ArtBook to Amsterdam's major museums means that it is frequented by curators, gallery directors, students and, of course, artists and writers. It is owned by the educational Dutch chain De Slegte, whose stores are filled with students purchasing their annual reading list or returning last year's books for the resale service. All the new art, architecture and design books are displayed from silver cupboards. The man responsible for these – and for the whole look of the store – was the architect Peter Sas. He designed all the furniture and bookshelves to be fairly minimal, the colour to be supplied by the books themselves and the luminescent tangerine ceiling.

COUTURE AND BOILER SUITS

22 Mart Visser Haute Couture

Paulus Potterstraat 30a

One of the Netherlands's leading couturiers, Mart Visser celebrated a decade of success in 2003. His appointment-only atelier and salon moved into a former bank, opposite the Van Gogh Museum, designed by Diederik Dam (son of Cees who was responsible for the Stopera building). He was honoured with a retrospective exhibition at the Gemeente Museum in Den Haag; at just 35 years of age, this is no mean feat for a man whose tailoring technique was honed in the atelier of the Netherlands's answer to Yves Saint Laurent, Frans Molenaar and Anne Klein in New York. Visser prides himself on his couture and dresses the most famous women in the country. His renown has resulted in international expansion and the Bagage, Chaussure, Belt, Bridalwear, Prêt à Porter and beach and resort-wear ranges will soon be available across Europe.

MIFFY THE RABBIT

23 The Nijntje Shop

Beethovenstraat 71

Nijntje is one of Holland's best-loved children's characters and best-known exports, instantly recognizable under the name Miffy. The Dutch rabbit is *konijn* and, with 'tje' added, connotes something 'small and sweet'. This girl bunny was the creation of Dick Bruna who won the Children's Book Award for *Nijntje in the Tent* in 1966. He is famous for characters that appear in over 100 picture books. The Nijntje Shop stocks most of his storybooks, along with all the other popular Bruna paraphernalia.

Zuidelijke Grachten
De Pijp
Plantage

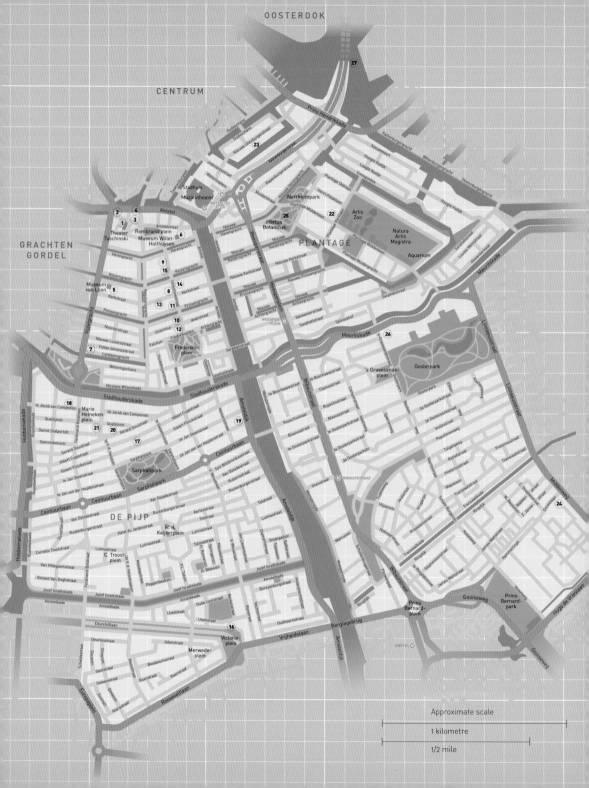

The density of entertainment on offer along Amsterdam's grand canals is such that the Vijzelgracht provides a useful (if somewhat artificial) division at this point. The southern stretch of the grand canals running from the Vijzelgracht (itself a former canal, but which was filled in to create larger roads) is part of the extension of the horseshoe shape that flanks the Centrum from the original *grachten gordel* (canal ring) and loops around to meet the Amstel River. Their grand façades are as imposing as the original north-western stretch and today they too house a mix of corporate and private residences. The meeting of the Herengracht and Reguliersgracht with its seven bridges was cut at the same time, and offers one of the city's most picturesque vistas through the arches of the *brug*. It is also the junction of the south-western corner of the Rembrandtplein, now a neon eyesore blighting the square that was once home to Amsterdam's butter market and which still holds the city's oldest statue of the Dutch master after whom the square was named in 1876. The characterless bars and cafés are just the obvious face of an area that is full of colloquial secrets. On the edge of the *plein* itself sits the gothic-inspired castle of the Theater Tuschinski (p. 82) and opposite is Amsterdam's latest 'private' members' club, Cineac (p. 82). Some of the best restaurants are hidden on first floors, so that unappealing punters will not wander in by mistake. The shops on Utrechtsestraat provide a taster of what is to come as you head on down to De Pijp.

The Vijzelgracht ends at an intersection dominated by a building close to many a Dutchman's heart: the Heineken Brewery was founded here in 1865 and provided a buffer between the *grachten gordel* extension and the less salubrious working-class neighbourhood of De Pijp. But its cheap rent and a post-Second World War influx of Surinamese and Indonesian immigrants have transformed this area into a strong social community based around Amsterdam's largest street market, the Albert Cuypmarkt. New bars and restaurants are opening up and on the streets near the stalls that sell the usual market fare are shops that are well worth a rummage. The hipness factor here is high, and De Pijp's metamorphosis from ethnic backwater to destination location for bright young things parallels that of Notting Hill in London or the Lower East Side in New York.

As the grand canals hit the Amstel so they meet the Plantage (plantation), so named because it was once a lush green suburb bordering farming fields that met the diamond factories at the edge of the old Centrum. It has retained a verdant character with the Hortus Botanicus (p. 90), Artis Zoo, the city Planetarium, Aquarium and Geological Museum, as well as some attractive eateries for digesting all the culture.

ART DÉCO CINEMA
1 Theater Tuschinski
Reguliersbreestraat 26–34

Jewish refugee Abraham Tuschinski's cinema is a decadent example of Art Déco architecture by Heyman Louis de Jong, with a kaleidoscopic interior decorated by Chris Bartels, Jaap Gidding and Pieter den Besten (sunglasses are recommended when viewing the original carpet). The house offers guided tours, current movie releases and classic silent films accompanied by live music from the Wurlitzer organ, harking back to its variety theatre heyday when Marlene Dietrich and Judy Garland played here. Sadly, Tuschinski was sent to Auschwitz in 1942, where he died.

INTERNATIONAL PRIVATE SOCIAL CLUB
2 Inez IPSC
124

PRIVATE ESTABLISHMENT
3 Cineac
Reguliersbreestraat 31

Astounding as it may be, architect J. Duiker's Cineac was built a mere decade after the Tuschinski. This early functionalist work (1934) more recently suffered the misfortune of being Amsterdam's Planet Hollywood. It was restored not long ago and Duncan Stutterheim opened it as one of Amsterdam's first private clubs. Historically, Amsterdammers are loath to accept private clubs, but Stutterheim just wants people to make more of an effort and provide somewhere for politicians and celebrities to feel at ease. The opulent interior by Wim van de Oudeweetering reflects the original red and silver colours of the building. A 40-metre-high projection ceiling and four levels of lounge and restaurants focusing on a centre-piece bar are surely reason enough to don suit or heels?

HOBBY HORSE
4 De Vlieger
Amstel 34–52

This stationery shop, dating from 1869, has loyal customers in their eighties, who have been coming here to buy paper, craft and hobby materials since before they could walk. It is crammed full of anything and everything connected with writing and hobbies: bookcase screws, ribbons, a selection of local paper, as well as handmade varieties from India, Nepal and Japan. The chaotic shop is spread over two floors and parts of it are often accessed via a stepladder.

5 Museum van Loon
Keizersgracht 672

In 1973 the aristocratic Amsterdam merchant family van Loon threw open their front door as an invitation to their home and family history. One of the first residents of the 17th-century house was Rembrandt's most renowned pupil, Ferdinand Bol. The architect Adriaan Dortsman built it in 1672 as one of a pair of symmetrical homes for the Flemish merchant Jeremias van Raey. During the 18th century the interior was clad with stucco and marble panelling and the staircase adorned with an elegant copper balustrade. The house is full of family portraits and scattered with silver and porcelain collections; Jacob de Wit's wall friezes feature in the upstairs rooms. It offers an impressive and elegant insight into a normally private aspect of privileged Amsterdam life.

GRAND TRADITION
6 Museum Willet-Holthuysen
Herengracht 605

Sandrina Willet-Holthuysen bestowed her family's 17th-century canal house on the city of Amsterdam when she died in 1895. The house on the *grachten gordel* (canal ring) was built in 1685 and acquired by her coal-magnate father, Peter Holthuysen, in 1855. The generous gift included the sizeable art collection of her late husband, Abraham Willet; both were keen collectors of silver, glass, ceramics and paintings. For over a century, the public have been able to enjoy the beautiful aristocratic Dutch house: a magnificent ballroom on the first floor, a dining and family drawing room that overlooks the garden, and the opulent blue room hung with heavy blue damask, with its central focus on the Jacob de Wit chimney-piece.

YOUNG INTERNATIONAL ART
7 Akinci
Lijnbaansgracht 317

Leyla Akinci opened her gallery in 1988 and the range of artists represented here is testimony to her respected position in the contemporary art arena. Chantal Joffe, who was part of New York Contemporaries in 1996, the German photographer Sonja Braas and the artist Thomas Schütte are just some of the names in her stable, along with local talent Ronald Versloot. Many of Akinci's protégés appear in significant international shows, Juul Hondius being a recent example with his photographic work exhibited at the Stedelijk Museum.

BAGS, BELTS AND BOOKS

8 JAN

Utrechtsestraat 74

Rutger Janssen and Janna Hallink used the common syllable in their names for the title of their shop. Together they created the small, white minimalist space and filled it with their choice of belts, jewelry, watches and toys. They also sell a trendy, functional selection of branded bags, which includes Freitag, Ortlieb and Manhattan Portage, alongside classic contemporary china by Rosenthal, cutlery by Iittala, coffee-table flick books and other perfect gifts for the hip home-loving thirty-something. JAN is the expression of their own favourite finds, and the space is kept selectively and aesthetically stocked.

GARDENER'S QUESTION TIME

9 Seeds of Passion

Utrechtsestraat 26

Henk van Dalen specializes in cannabis seeds. He enjoys a good reputation and long history in the Netherlands for quality cannabis-related products, and sells over 175 varieties from his shop and via his wholesale business, Dutch Passion. Seeds of Passion was renovated in 2001, but had previously operated as an outlet for hemp products, marketing cloth, food and drinks. The shop staff are willing to provide advice on the type of seed to suit each customer from a range that includes blueberry, sky walker, white widow and power plant.

THE CHRISTMAS TWINS

10 Backstage

Utrechtsedwarsstraat 67

Twin brothers Gary and Greg Christmas were vaudeville stars, dancing on the Broadway stage in their native America until they decided to settle in Amsterdam in 1971. They had always dreamed of owning a little shop and living above it, and in 1975 this came true for them with Backstage. They began selling handmade clothes, which Gary still loves to show to customers. Now Backstage is an eccentric café offering snacks and coffee. Sadly, Greg died but Gary, now in his seventies, is always ready to sit down and offer his positive and hilarious take on life to the regulars who frequent his tables.

NOT CHIPS
11 Fishes
Utrechtsestraat 98

Contemporary consumers are often confused by seafood, according to the brothers Philippe and Georgy Bedier de Prairie. They engaged the experience of the fish merchants Bart van Olphen and Chris Hogenbirk and agreed they wanted to break away from the feel (and smell) of traditional fish shops. Enter architect Paul Linse (of Schiphol Airport and the new Rijksmuseum extension), who designed a modern industrial shop to provide organic and wild fresh fish, prawns and lobsters. Fishes also sells all the condiments and cookbooks to guide the novice chef through their culinary options, as well as ready-cooked seafood meals.

TEA OR COFFEE?
12 De Plantage
Utrechtsestraat 130

Marleen Bakker wanted her customers to share her passion for the nation's favourite beverages and made sure that her shop selling tea and coffee offered good sampling opportunities. Her customers appreciate this and she has a loyal clientele who enjoy learning about the flavours and history of the bean and leaf. From green tea to lemon tea; mocha to Arabica, Bakker's stock is vast and varied.

ANTIPODEAN ADVENTURE
13 Moko
126

INDONESIAN SPICE ROUTE
14 Tempo Doeloe
130

OPEN LATE
15 Kitsch
Utrechtsestraat 42

This mad little restaurant's name holds the key to its décor and menu. Kick Woltjer opened it in 2000 when he was only 26 and filled it with Plexiglas, fake fur, 1970s posters and a clientele to match. The space is so small that it doesn't take much for conversation decibel levels to equal the groovy tunes he uses as aural backdrop. The restaurant provides 'everything from salad to lobster; from burgers to caviar'. Kick's attitude is fun and he is unusual in this city for keeping the kitchen open until 11pm on week nights and midnight at weekends.

This place must be seen for its size and structure alone. On the busy market street that is De Pijp's Albert Cuypstraat, Leo Coolen has opened an imposing restaurant-café named after the statue that hangs above the entrance. The building started life in 1951 as a church and was converted first into a supermarket and then into a record store before Coolen got his hands on it. He was an antique dealer by trade and there are hints of this throughout the vast, two-tiered space where gothic religious artifacts abound. Five spiky chandeliers, which were rescued from a Belgian casino, dangle ominously from the ceiling. The entrance and long bar originated in a Parisian musical theatre and Coolen found the upper-level restaurant railing in Egypt. He adds unpredictable flavour to the standard food by mounting experimental art projects on the walls and providing live classical music during Sunday brunch.

The city's botanical gardens began life as an apothecary's herb garden. The vegetation population was expanded by the arrival of ships from the Dutch East India Company, returning from formerly uncharted territory with their newly discovered seed varieties and tropical plants intended for medicinal use at the Hortus Medicus. Fifty years later, in 1682, it put down permanent roots on the Plantage Middenlaan. Some of the original specimens are still growing in the palm greenhouse, which was built in 1912. There are three other greenhouses with temperatures set to accommodate alternative climates: tropical, subtropical and desert. The gardens feature several varieties of Dutch tulip, flesh-eating plants, the Victoria Amazonica water lily and an Agave from the early 19th century, the oldest pot-plant in the world. Over 6,000 plant varieties constitute what has become one of the largest botanical collections in existence.

Some of Renzo Piano's best-recognized work has been in big statement buildings. The Pompidou Centre in Paris stands as a witness to his fearless expression on a huge scale. He designed Amsterdam's science and technology centre as an emerald and rust ship (it is actually copper-clad) that appears to emerge majestically 30 metres from the ground. This neat illusory trick is the result of a clever adaptation of the existing ramps of the IJ tunnel, which are used as the foundation of the museum. This means that a single truss keeps the entire structure vertical, a feat of engineering that completes the synergy of science, technology and art. Inside the centre children and adults alike can enjoy the demonstrations, performances and interactive exhibits, which enhance the educational environment.

Eilanden

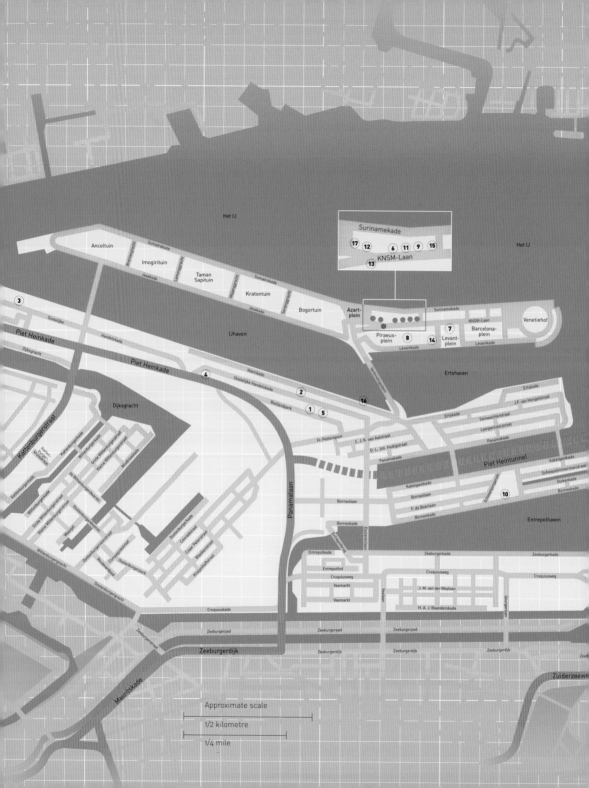

One of Amsterdam's biggest redevelopment projects has been taking place only two kilometres from Centraal Station. The docklands to the east of the city have undergone an extraordinarily skilful facelift, which has brought life and energy to a defunct area in the form of arrogant new architecture, galleries and huge contemporary design emporiums. What used to be one of the most isolated, desolate sections of the city has been revived and vitalized following a referendum that voted in favour of saving the old docks and building new residential spaces. Since 1990, over 8,000 residences have gone up on the Oostelijk Havengebied, which constitutes the four peninsulas or Eilanden (islands): Java-, KNSM-, Borneo-eiland and Sporenburg. As in much of Amsterdam, the feeling of overcrowding is dispelled thanks to the constant proximity of large scenic water vistas.

The docks – 140 hectares of land, 160 hectares of water – were constructed between 1876 and 1927 because the building of Centraal Station made the city's oldest harbour on the IJ inaccessible to large ships. Over time they themselves became too small to sustain the increasing size of ships and loads, and when the new harbour Westelijk Havengebied came into being the eastern docks suddenly had no purpose at all.

The first sign of redevelopment on the (soon-to-be-tram) route from the station is the new Passengers' Terminal by the Danish architects Hellmuth, Obata & Kassabaum, who have created a virtually transparent junction for water and land traffic with an undulating roof and balcony affording visitors a spectacular view across the IJ. The closest of the Eilanden can be accessed via the Jan Schaeferbrug, colloquially referred to as the 'Lizard Bridge' owing to the similarity of the steel supports to reptile legs. The western sector is Java-eiland and the eastern KNSM-eiland. Java's layout was planned by the eminent Amsterdam architect Sjoerd Soeters, who employed the services of a different architect every 27 metres, the result being a diversity of living spaces that reflect the real city centre. But the sexy social spine is KNSM-eiland, named for the Koninklijke Nederlandse Stoomboot Maatschappij (KNSM; Royal Dutch Steamboat Company) who erected the first buildings there. The architect and urban planner Jo Coenen, appointed chief government architect of the Netherlands in 2000, has overseen almost 3,000 residences in a space just 700 by 150 metres. Laying all carparks underground and gardens on rooftops overlooking one central road that punches straight down the backbone of KNSM-eiland, he maximized the spatial sense for all the architects' studios, interior-design stores and galleries that have moved into the former warehouses, turning a defunct space into the most desirable aspirational living 'mall' in town.

The hotel's 120 rooms, ranging – in price and style – from one to four stars, are located in the former Lloyd building, one of the most eagerly anticipated renovations of the Eilanden. Gerrit Groen, Otto Hah, Liesbeth Mijnlieff and Suzanne Oxenaar come from an art, theatre and restaurant/*horeca* background and have all played seminal roles in the development of Amsterdam's culture over the past three decades. As such, they arrived as project founders to open a hotel with an innovative perspective. The building was originally a hotel for Jewish immigrants (as they waited to emigrate to America), a prison and most recently artists' studios. Oxenaar was part of the concept clan behind the Supperclub (p. 151), Mijnlieff opened three restaurants (Amsterdam, Mijnlieff and Verkendam), Hah was an events organizer and Groen the financial brains of the project. The hotel is designed to house a variety of artistic and social ideas. Its egalitarian philosophy encompasses one-star mini cabin rooms, rooms with kitchens, four-star suites with their own entrance, self-contained maisonettes and a library. The hotel will provide equipment (slide-projectors, tables) for guests who wish to use their rooms as a workspace. Rem Koolhaas-trained architects Winy Maas, Jacob van Rijs and Nathalie de Vries (collectively known as MVRDV) are leading the restoration.

As a lover of water and space, self-styled artist Lucy Nooren saw an opportunity to make something out of nothing in a disused industrial glass building overlooking the IJhaven. The 400 square metres were too large for Nooren's projects alone, which have seen her delve into painting, drawing, photography and sculpture over the past 20 years. Since opening on Valentine's Day 2003, the gallery has proved a unique platform for young Dutch art, photography and fashion talent. Nooren curates four shows a year, which have included rising names such as Aico Dinkla (fashion couture), Ludwig Langvreugd (functional design for kids) and Irene Janze (drawing). The gallery also remains the outlet for her own brushwork.

Diederik Janssen and Esther Scheffer were squatting in the former quarantine quarters of the Lloyd shipping building when they had the inspiration to turn their home into a local canteen. They now live down the street and the space has undergone a design overhaul by the architects Customr (Willem van der Sluis and Hugo Timmermans). The ground floor is divided into a café-restaurant serving sandwiches, snacks and Asian cuisine and an art space – referentially named Quarantine – with a rotating exhibition schedule. The narrow railroad-style bar and inside tables are visually doubled and elongated by a mirror-clad wall. The rest of the building is let out as artists' studios. Several alternative uses of space and the proliferation of artists and works-in-progress in the gallery make De Cantine a nice local meeting point on this fast-changing stretch of the Eilanden.

When this gallery opened in 1985 KNSM-eiland was not the chic design mecca that it is today. The founder Josje de Baart was promoting a group of artists whom she had collected through her painter husband and her love of modern Western art. De Baart felt that she could not give them the necessary visual outlet without a proper space to show their work. Twenty years ago the surrounding area was derelict and it was hard to get people to venture out to an empty industrial harbour zone. Time has changed all that, and De Baart's tenacity has been the making of her gallery and the reputation of her artists.

7 Hair & Body Affairs

Levantkade 167

8 De Ode

Levantkade 51

Until recently Kees Jan owned the only hair salon on the Eilanden; now there is another, but he still has the only beauty parlour to fall under the banner of 'body' in his Hair & Body Affairs. Having sharpened his scissors at De Kapper (one of the city's best-known salon chains), Jan ventured out on his own at 25. Less than ten years on, he oversees a staff of ten and his salon has become an impromptu meeting point for locals as they get their hair cut, coloured or trimmed, nails polished, eyelashes tinted or make-up touched. Of course, the focus remains hair. And the client. Jan did spend time doing couture hair for the catwalk but realized that he wanted to concentrate more on his customers. The salon is always buzzing with news and the latest styles. The décor of warm lights reflecting off mirrors, styled by FG Stijl architects, creates a 'fresh feel' for your 'new look'.

Holland is known for its pragmatic attitude to many aspects of life, such as sex and drugs, which other nations struggle with. De Ode is an example of this ideology, the focus being death. Husband-and-wife team Nicola Capaan and Wouter Carpij used to design gravestones and monuments and wanted to bring a more intimate atmosphere to the funeral parlour by providing a customized service. Couture coffins are available in a variety of materials that may be hand-painted, upholstered or covered in turf. The couple spend time talking to the deceased's relatives so that the work they produce for the funeral is really a celebration of their life and memories. One example reflects the Dutch as a nation of cyclists: De Ode has created an attachment for a coffin, so that it can be fixed to the back of a bicycle and pulled to the cemetery.

A MESS IN THE HOUSE

9 Keet in Huis
KNSM-Laan 303

A stroller-friendly winding ramp spirals from street level into the split mezzanine of this funky and functional kids' store. Clothes, toys, books and accessories for both the pre- and post-natal periods are profiled in a non-prescription presentation that will appeal to the non-predictable parent (to be). The Keet label, developed by the owners Denise van Poppel and Door Fransen, provides birth cards, lighting, bedspreads, blankets and furniture. The two met whilst working for the successful Dutch children's clothing company Oilily, but after having kids of their own felt that there was room for a shop that combined the needs of the discerning designer and young mum. They were proved right and have recently opened a second store in Antwerp.

SEASIDE

10 De Oceaan
R.J.H. Fortuynplein 29 (Borneokade)

Michael Brinkman opened his first restaurant in 1999, making it fairly establishment as far as the Eilanden go. As its name suggests, the predominant dishes are seafood, but in keeping with modern international cuisine, Thai, Dutch and French elements have been added to the mix. It is located on the mainly residential and therefore quiet Borneokade, and as such has become the upmarket local for locals. Brinkman is responsible for his own brand range of wine and water, which can be enjoyed on the waterfront terrace all year round, thanks to a roof and outdoor heating.

11 Dominio
KNSM-Laan 301

The common factor in the selection of clothes, accessories and furniture at Dominio is their country of origin. Taco Joustra worked in Milan for 12 years before returning to his native Holland, where his love for Italian design resulted in this shop. Joustra has noticed that the Dutch affinity for all things French is slowly switching to all things Italian and he supplies the less obvious brands: 1950s ceramics by Bitossi (who once employed Ettore Sottsass), vintage espresso machines ranging from 1910 onwards (Joustra emphasizes that these are for decoration rather than use) and a Dominio men's fashion label collection.

NOT JUST POTS
12 Pol's Potten
KNSM-Laan 39

In a former cocoa-bean warehouse overlooking the River IJ is a vast space filled with household accessories and custom-made kitchens and units in which to store them. The product of three industrial designers – Eric Pol, Jan Wolleswinkel and Theo Grootendoorst – Pol's Potten is the outlet for the crockery, glassware and cutlery that they gather from jaunts to the Far East, mixed with objects found closer to home. They have used their space effectively: tall wood and steel shelves divide the area into narrow corridors, and colour, texture and shape are provided by the chunky glassware, delicate candelabras, plastic bowls and misshapen lights that cover them. The trio are well respected as witty trendsetters – a huge 'Verboden te Roeken' (no smoking) sign is painted across one of their beams – and they constantly change the look of their shop with the turnover of stock and ironic window displays.

BOUQUET BOUTIQUE
13 Art and Flowers
KNSM-Laan 6

Eduard Kortbeek and Marcelus Slaib de Souza have been combining art and floristry for 17 years from their shop in Muiden. The close friends were inspired by the rejuvenation on the Eilanden and moved premises there in 2002. Art and Flowers is another functional boutique along this stretch, in which vibrancy and contemporary graphics focus the eye and, in this case, the nose as well. They specialize in bringing together dead materials, such as Australian ghost wood, with bright, breathing flowers to emphasize the sculptural structure of flower arranging. They also make permanent garden sculpture; Hannah Delgorge's distressed marble torsos are a particularly popular form of outdoor art.

CAFÉ CULTURE
14 Kanis & Meiland
Levantkade 127

With a low-key terrace on the waterfront, Kanis & Meiland (the name is a pun on 'KNSM-Laan Eiland') is the Eilanden's most laid-back café. Owners Kees Reuf, Ed Schapers and Ronald van Binnen were already established in Amsterdam's local hospitality trade with their popular bar and restaurant, Café de Koe (Marnixstraat 381). Kanis & Meiland opened nine years ago and offers standard quality Dutch lunches, sandwiches, *tosties* (toasted sandwiches) and soups, light evening meals and all the usual beers, wines and spirits. The pool table and sea-faring décor are in keeping with the owners' good sense of humour.

ART LENDING FOUNDATION
15 SBK Amsterdam
KNSM-Laan 307–9

The Stichting Beeldende Kunst (Art Lending Foundation) was formed in 1955 with the aim of loaning art to its members. SBK's collection currently extends to over 50,000 works of art. The paintings, graphic art, sculptures, drawings and photographs are predominantly created by artists who live and work in the Netherlands, making it a powerful representation of national contemporary art. Selection is by an independent board and purchases are made directly from the artist. Over 1,000 Dutch artists regularly contribute art to the Foundation. This is one of 11 branches of SBK and its vast size means that the clientele is mostly corporate, as only they have the space to house the large pieces displayed.

RESTAURANT ON A SHIP
16 Odessa
131

RUST EN EENVOUD
17 Pilat & Pilat
155

Style Traveller

sleep • eat • drink
shop • retreat

sleep

The image of hotels is changing in this city, at last catching up with the refined design ethic for which the Dutch are renowned. This doesn't mean that you can't catch forty winks in an old canal house, but the canal house interior has been repackaged and now represents the latest innovation in style. The practical, functional, opulent or minimal use of space will provide respite and, in several bolt-holes, surprisingly more. Destination restaurants, libraries, even nightclubs are already part of the featured extras, and as ideas evolve, these eight are destined to be the trendsetters for a revolution in hospitality.

The fact that this hotel has an address for a name is the first clue that its aim is to be a 'home from home', as opposed to a hotel. Seven One Seven is undoubtedly about the personal touch. A flight of stairs leads from the imposing grandeur of street-level Prinsengracht to the front door of this classical 19th-century listed building where visitors must ring the doorbell and wait to be received before entering. The marble hallway leads into a library stocked with magazines and ornaments and the overstuffed furniture focuses around a fireplace. There is no visual clue that this is anything other than a private home. This was the intention of the original owner, Kees van de Valek, in the 18 months that he occupied and decorated the house before selling it – contents as seen – to its current proprietors, the Oyster Group. Each of the eight rooms (guaranteeing that there are never more than 16 guests in the hotel at any time) is unique and has a name hinting at the inspiration for its style. The Picasso suite is one of two with five tall windows overlooking the canal; its walls feature the work of the Spanish master. Guests sleep on handmade antique-style brass beds from Deptich Designs, covered in sheets by Westpoint USA and wrapped in blankets commissioned by the hotel from Melin Tregwynt of Wales. All rooms are equipped with Bang & Olufsen DVD and stereo systems and with a selection of music and movies. This 'extra' is inclusive in the room rate, as is breakfast, which can be taken in the dining room on the ground floor, on the patio or delivered in a picnic basket to the room. The complimentary courtesy extends to all drinks and food consumed on the premises (within reason) and substantiates the original ambition to create a home from home.

TOSTAY TONIGHT
80
Hotel Arena
26 's-Gravesandestraat 51
Rooms from €175

Paul Herminades's 121-room hotel is situated in the former St Elisabeth Chapel on the edge of Amsterdam's Oosterpark, which is home to the botanical gardens. Such a vast building is unusual in this densely populated city and, not surprisingly, the space was originally intended for more benevolent purposes. Opened in 1890 by Roman Catholics as a home for disabled people, it later housed orphans and finally geriatrics. By 1982 it was under the jurisdiction of the local government, which felt that the best use for the space would be as Amsterdam's biggest low-budget hostel; but by the end of the 1980s it had been privatized as Arena. Herminades became involved at this point as he worked with the Participatie Maatschappij voor Kunst en Kultuur ('participating company dedicated to art and culture'). In 1999 he transformed it again into the three-star Hotel Arena. Multifunctional by virtue of the on-site restaurant, bar, nightclub, terrace and garden, Arena has successfully combined the social and modern needs of a hotel without losing sight of the poignant history of the building. The restaurant and toilets (those in the nightclub light up as a warning when occupied) were designed by the local creative mastermind Ronald Hooft. High ceilings and long hallways dominate the interior and connect the sparse rooms. It will be up to the occupier to decide whether these are fashionably minimal or rather on the monastic side. The nightclub is intended as a convenient way for locals and tourists to mix and the hotel is frequently used for filming or as a backdrop for photo shoots. Arena has successfully created a youthful dynamic atmosphere that is reflected in its clientele.

70 Hotel Jan Luyken

3 Jan Luijkenstraat 58

Rooms from €200

One block from the Museumplein upon which sit the Van Gogh Museum, the Stedelijk and the Rijksmuseum, the Hotel Jan Luyken is a quiet former family home named after the street on which it is situated. Jan Luyken was Holland's most famous illustrator and poet at the turn of the 18th century. He illustrated *The Trades of Man* in 1694 and this work still appears frequently as a decorative motif on wrapping paper and business cards in the Netherlands. In the 19th century the physiotherapist J.J.W. van Schaik ran his practice from his home on this street. His brilliant reputation brought him clients from around the world and to compensate for the lack of local accommodation he converted part of his house into rooms for them to stay in. As his client base grew, he acquired the houses on either side of his own and so completed the three-house hotel that exists today. His children continued the business after his death, but recently sold it to the Dutch Bilderberg group who are restoring it as a contemporary boutique hotel with traditional touches. Etienne Bouten of B&B Design has renovated the 62 rooms and installed huge shower heads and striped coloured wallpaper. A bold use of reds and greens contrasts with the white of the base palette and extra attention to detail is given in the form of CD players and flowers. A mini day spa offers massages or access to a jacuzzi, shower-steam room and the inevitable sunbed. Separate to the breakfast area is an incognito bar with a selection of half-bottles of wine and appetizers. Throughout the space, the paintings (gifts given to van Schaik by grateful clients), old fireplaces and some breathtaking examples of original Art Déco tiling remain, but the furniture and accessories are new.

70 **Blaine's B&B at the Park**

15 Gerard Brandstraat 14hs
Rooms from €130

Blaine Hamrick's began working in the hospitality industry in his native USA and he went to Asia before arriving in Amsterdam in the mid-1990s. He started his bed-and-breakfast establishment with Blaine's B&B at the Park, located on the perimeter of the Vondelpark. The three rooms were designed by Bob Saretsky, the original owner of the house, and each breathes its own style. The garden room is the largest and overlooks Blaine's flowering backyard; the Wedgwood room combines Amsterdam School and Baroque decorations with contemporary furniture; and the Portrait room houses a collection of portraits by Saretsky. Blaine's experience with an international hotel chain provides a guarantee of high-quality service on this smaller scale. Breakfast can be taken in the dining room or garden and he is also amenable to providing dinners and even dinner parties on request. The success of this venture led Blaine to expand and the B&B now extends to ten rooms in three venues: Blaine's B&B at the Park, Blaine's B&B and Peter's B&B. In 2001 Blaine teamed up with his Dutch partner Peter Waltz, and their latest venture is a restaurant in the centre of town.

17TH-CENTURY GRANDEUR

48 **Canal House Hotel**

7 Keizersgracht 148
Rooms from €170

The Canal House Hotel is just as its name suggests: a hotel in a grand old 17th-century Dutch house located on the prestigious Keizersgracht. The owners Brian and Mary Bennett had been presiding over the successful micro-hotel Number 31 in Dublin for many years, when they found themselves drinking in the Canal House Hotel bar with its previous proprietors. They were Americans who had undertaken to restore the house when they first acquired it in the 1960s, and had since opened it to the public as a hotel. Brian Bennett mentioned over a drink that he wasn't averse to making them an offer, should they ever wish to sell, and the next thing Mary knew, she was running a 26-room establishment in the heart of Amsterdam. The original deeds of the house date back to 1640 and many of the patrician features are still apparent: the narrow front leading to the water and narrow corridors with high ceilings running the length of the house and opening into an elegant drawing room overlooking a lush green garden. This now doubles as a dining room and houses a grand piano, classic fireplace and mirrors; guests are served breakfast here. Luxurious panelling, plasterwork, more fireplaces and mirrors are found throughout the hotel's unusual layout. Reflective of the lack of space in this city, it practically wraps itself around another house and some of the rooms are reached by climbing up or down little private staircases at the end of slim hallways. The rooms themselves are comfortable and retain the 17th-century theme, with bare beams holding up the roof of the attic floor. The higher the storey, the more cramped the space becomes, but the eccentric asymmetry of the rooms is appealing. The ground-floor bar is very seductive and oozes dangerous charm.

ART HOTEL

14 **Winston**

28 Warmoesstraat 129
Rooms from €90

The Warmoesstraat used to be a seedy backstreet and the Winston a low-budget backpackers' paradise. Times have changed. While the street is still situated on the edge of the red-light district, it has been repaved and cleaned up. And so, in a manner of speaking, has the hotel. Aldert Mantje and Andre Mesman are both artists who have been working in public spaces for the past three decades. Mantje paints and once belonged to the notorious art collective Seymour Likely, who named their performance-art nightclub after this imaginary artist; Mesman is a visual installation artist. Their work outside of the white cube brought them to the attention of Frans Verlinden who wanted to provide a more structured environment for their creations to grow organically. He owned the Winston and extended it in 1995, installing them as creative directors in 1997. From this position they formed a link between the design colleges and visual artists of the Netherlands and the commercial arena. Every year they run competitions in the art academies, offering winners the opportunity to realize their design in a hotel room. Armed with a small budget (€500–700), the students have styled rooms that explore the idea of space through lighting, minimalism, a Cuban monk's cell complete with robes and an inspiring use of provocative photography. Mantje and Mesman also operate with large brands such as Heineken, Smirnoff and Durex, all of whom have sponsored rooms, so increasing the budget and profile of the designer. Hugo Kaagman is the well-known name behind the Heineken room, which combines a contemporary Dutch brand with traditional Dutch imagery. Most recently, Willum Geerts produced controversial images for the ground-level bar. Mesman emphasizes that it is not high art and the hotel is low budget. But to stay at the Winston is a unique opportunity to immerse oneself in an energetic, evolving contemporary art project.

When the American and Canadian jeeps came rolling into Amsterdam and liberated the city at the end of the Second World War, the general feeling of jubilation caused this square to be christened 'Victorie'. The hostel opened there shortly afterwards and took its name from the location as 'Pension Victorie'. It remained small (with only four rooms) until it was bought by the Espinosa family in 1970. Over three decades their passion for hotels and, according to Tom Espinosa, 'accessible design without attitude' has turned it into a modern boutique hotel. The lobby is light and focuses around a pebble-dashed fireplace. Fresh flowers and a blackboard featuring the philosophy of the day attest to the vibrant youthful energy that dominates the environment. The generic area and 24 rooms were designed by Mirjam Espinosa with Ronald Hooft consulting. This has resulted in rubber-clad floors and walls, which are indistinguishable from slate. The breakfast bar is a huge free-standing open cabinet overflowing with bread, cheese, fruit, cold meats and the inevitable *hagelslag* (chocolate sprinkles, which the Dutch have been lavishing on their buttered bread since kindergarten). Mirjam, Tom and Jacqueline retain a hands-on approach to the day-to-day running of the hotel – and live there too – which elevates their hospitality to a reassuringly personal level.

THE OLD ALMSHOUSE

48 **Blakes**
22 Keizersgracht 384
Rooms from €370

Blakes was opened by British designer and hotelier Anouska Hempel in 1999 and completed a trio of small luxury establishments under her banner (the Hempel and Blakes in London being the others). It also marked her first venture onto the international stage. Since then, it has become one of the city's landmark hotels for quality service and privacy. The site on which the hotel stands has a rich history dating back to 1612, when the building of Amsterdam's fifth canal ring extension commenced. Five years later Samuel Coster bought the land and there founded the Duytsche Academie theatre. The profits were donated to local orphanages to avoid religious disapproval. In 1632 the architect Jacob van Campen was responsible for the stone theatre and he rose to further renown soon after with Amsterdam's town hall, which is now the Royal Palace on the Dam. For the theatre's centennial celebration Vivaldi personally conducted the permanent orchestra, and visitors have included the Prince of Orange, the King of Poland and the Tsar of Russia. But in 1772 the complex burned down and the only remaining original structure is the doorway. The site was sold to the regents of the most important Catholic charity of the day, who built a bakery there to feed the poor. Today, that bakery is Blakes restaurant. The food stocks, where people once queued for the bread, have become the lounge and the old alms room is now a bar. Hempel has preserved the historical feel of the building but blended it with her style of elegance and temperate use of colour throughout the 41 rooms. No two are the same, and all contrast east and west, black and white, old and new. She uses natural elements such as wood, stone, glass and cotton, creating a sense of calm throughout the hotel. Personal details are added in the jet-lag tea, oxygen canisters and her own brand of grapefruit soap and candles.

eat

Dutch cuisine may not play a leading role on the international gastronomic stage, but it doesn't follow that the Dutch are any less demanding when it comes to food that will appeal first to the eyes and then to the belly. In fact, the lack of national dishes means that their chefs have embraced the fashion for fusion and are producing radical plate art. Restaurateurs are also highly inventive in terms of design and location and all successfully infuse decadent ambience into whatever culinary creation they aspire to.

80 **Inez IPSC**

2 Amstel 2

The story of this restaurant will forever be a part of Amsterdam art and *horeca*/club culture. It was opened for Inez de Jong in 1998 by her husband, Peter Giele, as their next project, after years of running the legendary Roxy nightclub. Giele was an artist and part of the AORTO art collective with Aldert Mantje (now a creative director of the Winston hotel [p. 116]), but he died shortly after Inez IPSC opened. Some of his sculptures were made using extreme heat and fire (a photo of him forms the cover of the house match-books), and during his funeral wake the Roxy strangely burned down, watched by Inez and their friends from the new restaurant across the Singel. The end of the Roxy era heralded a new one for Inez. Her generation was getting older and had upped the stakes; conversation and good dining in a rococo-style room was starting to have more appeal than dancing till 6 am. Inez IPSC is hidden up a staircase off the Muntplein and the corner of the first-floor restaurant commands an inspiring view. The interior, a celebration of vibrant colour, bears testimony to Giele's creativity.

As with some of the other concept-club experiences in Amsterdam, Blender is set slightly off the beaten track but is well worth the detour for a guaranteed smart Amsterdam night out, as none of the guests will be tourists who have accidentally fallen in. It was opened in 2000 by Marcel Geurts, Remco Schigf and Edo Kamping (who cut his culinary teeth as the head chef at Bordewijk [p. 40] for six years), and combines restaurant with bar with club with lounge. Gilian Schrofor and Rob Wagamans at Concrete moulded the astounding interior in an acid array of contrasting colours. A 30-metre curving bar is the main focus of the space. This glazed tangerine feature forms the divider between Eames lounge chairs in the 28-seat restaurant and clementine Artifort chairs in the lounge. On the canal side a silver opaque curtain softens light cascading from the terrace. Food is good, French and Mediterranean, but the main reason to be here is the groove. And the toilets come in five colour varieties to suit your mood as the evening progresses: from bright yellow, pink, green, red and finally blue.

80 **Moko**

13 Amstelveld 12

Named after a Maori tattoo, Moko aims to bring a flavour of Australasian style and sensibility to a busy European city. Louis Rust's and Fred van Beusekom's aim was blessed with this location, as part of their scene (at least in the warmer months) is played out under trees on a vast terrace overlooking a playground. The site was reserved for the Amstel church in 1670, and a temporary building was erected as the herald of a huge Catholic cathedral that never actually materialized. These plans meant that nothing was ever constructed on the prime real estate. In the 19th century Amsterdam fell within the French Empire and Napoleon reserved the site for his stables, which were never built either. By the end of the 1980s, it was restored as a restaurant, which evolved into Moko in 2001. The chef worked in Australia and an accent is noticeable in the marinades and sauces. Inside, photos of New Zealand adorn the walls and there is a bamboo motif throughout by Niek Zwartjes; the terrace combines a laid-back outdoors Aussie–Balinese groove.

MOROCCAN KITCHEN

80 **Mamouche**

20 Quellijnstraat 104

There is a large Moroccan population in the Netherlands, most of whom have settled closer to Rotterdam than to Amsterdam. Farid Asserte has been living here on and off for over 23 years and had already established himself as a hairstylist with his own salon, Le Souk, located in the Negen Straatjes, before he opened this restaurant in 2002. So stunning are the subdued interior and the thought that has gone into the font and graphic design detail of the menus and signage that Asserte and fellow designer Steph Bakker were awarded the Dutch Design Prize for house style. The walls are smothered in raw plaster and their stormy hue is offset by the warmer tones of copper-foil-wrapped wenge wood furniture. Bakker is an experienced designer and was part of the first DKNY interior line alongside *Elle Deco* ex-editor, Ilse Crawford. Mamouche is also winning acclaim for its cuisine and Asserte insists on traditional ingredients such as couscous cooked in rosewater, dressed with fine almond oil from Ergane and tossed with unlikely sea-bass.

34 **Café-Restaurant Amsterdam**

3 Watertorenplein 6

Twenty-two floodlights that once lit stellar soccer moments at the Ajax and Olympic stadiums now shine down on the diners at Amsterdam. A former water pumping station built in 1897 was converted into a restaurant-café in 1996 by Liesbeth Mijnlieff who owned two other restaurants, Mijnlieff and Verkendam. She is no longer involved with Amsterdam, but can be found over on the Eilanden as part of the team behind the Lloyd Hotel (p. 96). Her visionary flair for egalitarianism inspired a menu that was designed to appeal to all. Expressed as a democratic restaurant, it features dishes that would have something for everyone, whether dining on budget or expense account. Considered one of the most beautiful industrial buildings in the country, it still carries clues to its former function, not least in the looming diesel engine next to the bar and the interior's vast size, which has made this a totally child-friendly environment.

70 **Vakzuid**

8 Olympisch Stadion 35

A restaurant in the old Olympic Stadium, interior designed by the sensational architect Paul Linse (whose shark-filled aquarium mesmerizes travellers at Schiphol Airport) and run by two of Amsterdam's best-loved restaurateurs, Philippe and Georgy Bedier de Prairie: all of this is Vakzuid ('section south'). In 1928 Amsterdam hosted the first-ever Olympic games in which women competed and this stadium was built by De Stijl founder architect Jan Wils. People still train there today, now overlooked by the diners and dancers of fabulous Vakzuid. Split over four levels, the establishment comprises a lounge terrace, dance area, subterranean cocktail lounge, restaurant and a private suite for business or parties. The vivacity of its owners and their vision of a concept club with such unusual dimensions have won them a gold in entertainment definition from the affluent, connected crowd that they pull in. It is a haunt of the fashionocracy who come to be seen or to eat the exquisite Indonesian fusion cuisine by master chefs Andy Tan and Volef Geboers.

48 **Pygma-Lion**
49 Nieuwe Spiegelstraat 5a

Dutch and South African histories have been intertwined for centuries, perhaps in ways that many would rather forget. It was not so long ago that Afrikaans was 'the language of the oppressor'. But as with any colonial rule, each party takes the richness of the other's culture and transplants it within their own. The South African Matthias Kleingeld has done just this with food in his wittily named restaurant, Pygma-Lion. His use of exotic ingredients in traditional family recipes could mean embarking on a culinary safari where crocodile, antelope and zebra are served up with more mundane vegetable accompaniments. Brie and coconut ostrich kebabs, zebra frikhandel or crocodile steak with wild-fruit chutneys are just a few examples of the combination of cultures found in the (melting) pot. Kleingeld wanted to expose the 350-year-old fusion kitchens of his birthplace to a more refined European palate in an environment whose style and ambience provided *kuierplek*, 'a little piece of home', in which to learn about the wines and food of his homeland.

80 **Tempo Doeloe**

14 Utrechtsestraat 75

Tempo Doeloe literally means 'the good old times' and presumably refers to those times when the Dutch imperialists ruled Indonesia as a colony outpost. The imposing regime brought back the best of flavours and recipes to the motherland, where they could be savoured by all. Tempo Doeloe has been serving traditional Indonesian cuisine for more than 14 years and represents the genuine rather than the fashionable in terms of food. The restaurant is presided over by Mr Ghabriel who has decorated the small yet cosy space with Indonesian puppet dolls, artifacts and flowers. But people come to here to eat, not to hang out or check out. Tempo Doeloe's homage to the smorgasbord comes in the form of a *rijst tafel* (rice table) and anyone who has not yet acquired the 'traditional' tastes of Indonesian cuisine should be warned that a sharp lesson will be played out on their tongue in a red-hot-chilli-pepper dance if guidance from the waitress is not heeded.

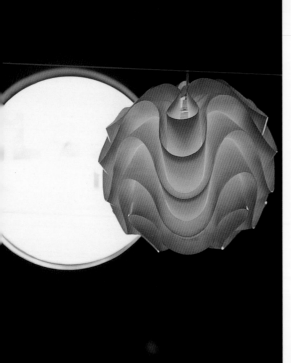

Jorica Koppen and Marit Weddepohl are responsible for Amsterdam's only super-trendy traditional Dutch eaterie. They acquired the restaurant in its former guise as De Blauwe Hollander (The Blue Dutchman), but to reflect their own ages, sense of style (Marit used to work in the Supperclub [p. 151] and at Madame Jeanette [p. 146] and Koppen's family have owned a restaurant for 25 years), and hair colour, they renamed it De Blonde Hollander. If you ever wondered what typically Dutch fare actually consists of, their menu provides the answer. Cheese croquettes with fried parsley, baked chicory with ham and cheese, salad of Texel lamb (from the largest Waddenzee island) and marrowfat peas with bacon and onion. It is certainly hearty food, but is served in contemporary surroundings. For dessert they really go to town on the nostalgia factor and offer a food close to the heart of anyone who grew up in Holland in the form of *poffertjes*, tiny deep-fried dough balls sprinkled with icing sugar.

The owners Koen van de Berg (who is also behind the tapas bar Pilsvogel in De Pijp) and Ramses Reijnaert threw down Odessa's plank to the public in 2001 and serve French Mediterranean cuisine to a hip local clientele. This genuine ship's hull was salvaged from a Ukrainian fishing boat and dates back to the 1920s. The Dutch duo teamed up with the New Zealand designer Corrine King to produce the surprisingly spacious dining area inside the hull. She transformed the interior using artful lighting and digital photo-print-panelled walls. These landscape images create an illusion of the outdoors in the restrictive dimensions of the surroundings. In the warmer months seating is extended up to the deck with room for about 140 people and enhanced with DJs, dancing and a Sunday barbecue. The cocktail bar remains popular in the colder winter months. But all year round Odessa manages to remain the Eilanden's seen/be seen eaterie and the novelty of eating on a boat just doesn't wear off.

14 De Bakkerswinkel
27 Warmoesstraat 69

An old tea warehouse has been transformed by the Bakkerswinkel crew into a huge lunchroom serving high teas from trolleys overflowing with cakes and a continually evolving selection of quiches, pies and condiments from the on-site kitchen located in what was once the old porter's lodge. De Bakkerswinkel's quiche plate (there are at least two choices daily), so often a nondescript snack elsewhere, resembles a giant slice of crumbling gateau perched on a mountain of green lettuce. Cake is also served in slabs rather than slivers and ranges from chocolate cheese to moist carrot. The lunchroom is large enough to host several parties simultaneously under one roof and has seating for up to 50 people in a private room at the back, which looks like an octogenarian's salon. It is an attractive place to stop for refreshment and its unassuming façade makes what is hidden within even more of a charming surprise.

POMP AND SPLENDOUR
48 Pompadour
17 Huidenstraat 12

Bram Ouwehand and partner Escu Ghabriels have been serving celebrated patisserie from this cosily decadent 'tea shoppe' since 1990. They acquired the site as a chocolaterie, which was founded in 1960, and turned it into the renowned establishment it is today with skills that Ghabriels developed as chef for the Belgian chocolatiers Leonidas. Every year the couple make sweet-toothed pilgrimages to Fauchon in Paris for training and return bearing new secret recipes such as passion-fruit crème with rare Tahitian vanilla. Popular appreciation is visible, as their wares often sell out early in the day. Pompadour also receives royal patronage and makes regular deliveries to the Royal Palace. Although Queen Beatrice herself has not been seen supping in the Fortuna-papered, wood-panelled tearoom, her sister Irene was for a long time a regular customer.

80 De Taart van m'n Tante

18 1e Jacob van Campenstraat 35

A humorous name for an amusing cake shop that is the creation of Siemon de Jong and Noam Offer. They started making pastries for the grand cafés of the city over 13 years ago and colluded with local artists to bake provocative, bizarre, yet always delightful cakes. This innovative attitude gained them a nationwide reputation and now the Royal Dutch House of Orange and native celebrities number among their regular clientele. Their renown has spread so far that Siemon himself has become a celebrity in his own right with a TV show where he builds cakes with kids while they engage in 'deep conversation'. The custom-made couture cakes are available in their colourful Konditorei. The colour scheme is icing-inspired and the sometimes sickly hues add childish fun to the eating of cakes. Summer 2003 also saw the opening of a B&B above the store: 'Cake Under My Pillow'. The mind boggles, but what better place to savour gateaux?

FOOD FOR THE PEOPLE

 Café de Jaren

 Nieuwe Doelenstraat 20–22

One of the largest and most unusual cafés in Amsterdam, spread over three levels and two terraces, Café de Jaren has long been a fixture meeting point. There is no doubt that it is already a well-known rendezvous, but the double-storey interior and simplicity of décor, spelled out in brown, cream and blue tiling and wooden functional furniture, make it a popular choice and it should be seen. In the warmer months seating spills onto a huge waterfront terrace and a first-floor balcony. Both overlook this amphibian-traffic-logged stretch of the Amstel. The café's relaxed attitude means that regulars can sit and enjoy a solitary coffee and read the papers for hours without having to order more. Before Café de Jaren started selling huge salads (from an impressive buffet on the first floor), snacks and drinks, this building was a bank. In the mid-1990s it was acquired by the brothers René and Fred Boerdan, who are building up an eaterie empire that currently includes Walem (p. 144) and Het Paleis.

LUNCH ALL DAY

NEWDELI

LUNCH ALL DAY

When it opened in 1997, Jacob Admiraal's *horeca* was a refreshing concept in Amsterdam. Modelled on media-savvy food bars more common in New York and London than Amsterdam, Admiraal teamed up with the creative mastermind Ronald Hooft, and their desire to express design as an international language is manifested through a primal white colour base, wenge wood tables, a stainless-steel bar and a shock-red stairwell. Clocks set to the time of transatlantic megalopolises add pace and vibrancy to an inevitably buzzy environment, where lunch is served all day. Admiraal had previously managed 'events concepts' at the Westergasfabriek (p. 37) during its peak of popularity in the mid-1990s. He bit into the *horeca* club sandwich with LOF (p. 44) in 1995 (now sold to Sander Louwerens) and has opened a second New Deli on the strength of the first. Like many such success stories, Admiraal now consults as a concept marketing strategist, but his global media dreams remain inherent in the 'new' design of New Deli.

70 **Spring**

5 Willemsparkweg 177

Ralph Woerde worked as a chef in this restaurant for three years before buying it for himself in spring 2003. He has a solid training that includes four kitchens in Holland with five Michelin stars between them. His culinary basis is in 'good fresh products' and he loves cooking seafood, as he thinks that 'fish is honest and healthy'. The sand-coloured linear design with vault-like glass façade windows overlooking the street is by Concrete. The view outside is usually obscured by a striking flower sculpture courtesy of the florist Menno Kroon (p. 158), who is conveniently located across the street. Woerde thinks the designers' pièce de resistance is the toilets, encased in solid gold fibreglass, which glow with an amber hue. He has another kitchen and private dining room on the first floor, where he offers more exclusive dinner party catering and personal cookery classes.

FRESH FOOD, FRESH IDEAS

80 **De Kas**

24 Kamerlingh Onneslaan 3

'Let's start a restaurant in a greenhouse' was the reaction of Gert Jan Hageman in 1995 as he bit into his first sun-ripened tomato from friend Walter Abma's nursery on the Purmer Polder. In 2001 his dream came true when the former municipal nursery of Amsterdam threw open its glass doors as the organic food restaurant De Kas. Hageman heard that the council had plans to tear down their 8-metre-high glass nurseries and was able to make his move. He managed to retain the original girders, and friends and family planted the first 5,000 seedlings. The architectural result is a refreshing excess of space, height and light. His team, like his concept, is strong and original. Abma oversees the produce on-site and on their land on the Purmer Polder, where seasonal vegetables are harvested outdoors: herbs and mediterranean vegetables in the summer and various types of lettuce in the winter. The chef Ronald Kunis was formerly at London's River Café and Hageman himself earned the restaurant Vermeer its first Michelin star as its chef in 1993.

48 **Christophe**

37 Leliegracht 46

This is Amsterdam's most famous French restaurant. Jean-Christophe Royer has one Michelin star and worked his way up the food chain, starting kitchen life washing dishes at the Ritz in Paris and eventually graduating with a full set of culinary tools from Aurora in New York. He came to the Netherlands to settle in 1987 and opened an establishment bearing his name. His food is influenced by his own origins as an Algerian-born Frenchman and he combines Mediterranean and Moroccan essences in an inherently southern French kitchen. The terrine foie gras, lobster and crème brûlée are some of his most celebrated dishes; the ragout of lobster cocoa beans, pimentos and coriander a more inventive one. The venue itself is an old building restyled by the American William Katz. The walls are covered in art by Christophe's contemporaries, set in a timeless interior that is modern but warm. Food is definitely the focus here.

80 **Altmann**

19 Amsteldijk 25

Arne Altmann opened this classy restaurant and bar in 2002 after starting off as a concierge at Blakes hotel (p. 121). The influence of his former employer can be detected in his own establishment: high-quality food and service, but also the mature atmosphere and subtle use of dark stone and soft lighting. Chocolate-coloured tables are silhouetted against light walls, and the restaurant is divided into a curving banquette near the bar and the main dining area. Separate to this is a raised level for 'public dining' where sitters have a better vista over the quietly buzzing environment. Altmann is located in a listed building, a renovated 19th-century bathhouse – formerly a carpark – that he and his stylist girlfriend converted into this sleek lobby, cocktail bar and restaurant serving global cuisine by another ex-Blakes employee, the chef Mohammed Mahroui. The menu changes daily, but sporadically features tabouleh with grilled vegetables and an aubergine feta mousse, tuna carpaccio with summer beetroot and ginger-soy dressing.

drink

Compared with the rest of the Continent, kitchens close early in Amsterdam, but bars stay open till late, at least 1 am on week nights and often till 3 am or later at the weekend. As many of the key watering holes also have kitchens they are really restaurant-bars. Yet it is the very fact that it is the norm just to get a drink, with maybe a snack, in a restaurant that makes drinking in Amsterdam such a sophisticated experience in the contemporary bars. The newer venues were a reaction to the notorious 'brown bars' (named for the nicotine-stained walls), old public houses with their own long rich history based on a national love of beer and booze.

Number One Zeedijk is one of the oldest buildings in the city and one of only two original wooden structures still standing in Amsterdam's city centre. The Zeedijk recently underwent a facelift in the form of repaving, but for a long time it was a notoriously sleazy street, wrapping around the east side of the red-light district and a second home to drug addicts. In 't Aepjen started life as a sailor's hostel in 1550 and the innkeeper was generous enough to permit seamen who had gambled or drunk their money to pay him with the monkeys they had brought back from their travels. Soon the hostel became a haven for apes and parasites. The sailors who slept there were identifiable because they were always scratching, having stayed 'in the monkeys'. This notion has filtered into the language as a colloquialism; the Dutch now refer to people in trouble as *in de aap gelogeerd*, which translates as 'stayed in the monkey'. The reason for In 't Aepjen's longevity is partly its rich history, but also its warm and mellow tones as a perfect backdrop for a *beertje* ('little beer').

About 350 different types of whisky are a good reason to visit De Still. The name is of course a play on the word distillery; *de still* in Dutch means 'the quiet', and *stillen* 'to quench' – in this case, a thirst. Jeroen Kruisheer and Bastiaan van der Staak took over De Still in 2003 having already worked there for several years. The bar opened in the early 1990s and has changed ownership a few times but has always had the love and support of its regulars and other local *horeca* people (they once clubbed together to save the bar when its original owner could no longer run it for health reasons), as it is a unique place in Amsterdam. For those who want to develop their palate the bar will arrange tasting sessions. There are the famous malts such as Macallen, Glenfiddich and Highland Park (who even provided the banquette at the back of the bar), alongside lesser known, rarer flavours from Old Pulteney and the house favourite, an Islay whisky distilled on a little island off Scotland called Caol Ila.

OLD BUT NEW

48 **Morlang**

43 Keizersgracht 451

Named after the psychological drama *Morlang* that was written here by the film's director Tjeboo Penning, this designer bar – and restaurant – is split over two levels. Stone steps lead up to the rococo façade and entrance is through a heavy red velvet curtain that arcs over the door and, in true New York style, protects customers from blustery weather outside. A linear bar divides the long space and a leather banquette faces the bar wall, lit up by soft caramel and sugar hues of spirit-, grain- and grape-filled bottles. Sjoerd Schneider owns the bar and now lives in New York, where she has cashed in on her Dutch cachet with an Atlantic twin, appropriately named the NL Bar. A spiral staircase leads down to the subterranean restaurant and the all-day menu mixes great salads with Indonesian spicy soups. Morlang has staying power and, being so close to the busy shopping alley of Leidsestraat, is well on the beaten track; yet it retains an exclusive allure, probably thanks to the tempered balance of a contemporary watering hole in a grand old Dutch canalside building.

80 Plancius

22 Plantage Kerklaan 61a

Hans van Twist's and Dick Spanje's names are already known to Amsterdam, because for many years they combined them for two cafés, Spanje van Twist. One of the cafés still exists near the Anne Frank Huis, although it is no longer under their control. The two pals met at college 20 years ago and pursued other careers before launching themselves in *horeca* culture. Plancius is impressively located in an old diamond-cutting factory (1860), which was remodelled for its current purpose by Merx&Girod, famous as the architects of the Concertgebouw and the new look of Hema (Holland's upmarket answer to Woolworths). A hundred square metres are filled with original exposed metal supporting girders that break up the dark slate, purple moleskin walls and wooden furniture. The moody colours are lightened by the crimson bar background, and exposed heating elements glow from the ceiling. This laid-back café is a real discovery in an area dominated by some busy tourist attractions, such as the zoo (which is opposite) and the Hortus Botanicus (p. 90).

48 **Walem**

42 Keizersgracht 449

The classic geometry of steel lines set at 90-degree angles and dividing panels of glass create the façade of a canal-view building on the grand old Keizersgracht that could only be the work of Gerrit Rietveld. It is the public face of what claims to be Amsterdam's first designer bar. Walem has certainly been around for a while and, although the décor and ownership have changed, the façade and industrial Rietveld staircase in the centre of the restaurant (which leads to the loos) have not. Brothers René and Fred Boerdan, who also own Café de Jaren (p. 134), added it to their stable over five years ago. The effect of the granite and wood interior is softened if you sit in the large terraced garden out back or at one of the few canalside tables that are placed in the sunshine in warmer months. Located next door to Morlang (p. 142), the two are inevitably busy, and customers dart between them waiting for the best table. Walem has managed to remain the occasional playground of Dutch soap opera stars and local glitterati.

POPE'S ISLAND

34 **Café 't Papeneiland**

15 Prinsengracht 2

This place will seem local even to those who have never been to Amsterdam before. A cosy bench and three tables on the ground floor, with a precarious mezzanine balancing above, crowd the tiny bar and its stalwart regulars who squeeze closer to the walls and smile, or grimace, every time a new face enters. Despite the huge black lettering 'Roken is dodelijk' ('smoking is deadly') plastered across cigarette packets, the concept that smoking is bad for your health does not seem to have hit home yet to many Dutch people and the bar is eye-wateringly smoky and noisy with the chatter of eccentric drinkers. Café 't Papeneiland has top high-novelty factor. Along with the beers and speciality *jenevers* (Dutch grain-based gin) the proprietor serves hard-boiled eggs as a 'stomach liner'. It also has historical value as the fourth oldest brown bar, built in 1642, and was once a funeral parlour bootlegging beer, with a secret passageway running from its cellar to a house on the opposite side of the canal. Perhaps ironically, it emerges at number 7 where a secret chapel once stood.

DRINKS AWAY!

14 **Kapitein Zeppos**

42 Gebed Zonder End 5

Being hidden up a very missable alleyway is a useful way to give drinkers at Kapitein Zeppos the feeling that they are off the beaten track and have discovered an alcoholic underbelly of Amsterdam. In fact they have, as the average Amsterdammer will also have failed to notice this gem of a bar (named after a famous Belgian television star of the 1960s), despite the fact that it is located at the heart of the Amsterdam university complex and just off Nes, the city's main promenade for fringe theatre. As such, this place is perfect for a quiet drink, and the bar will make both the solitary drinker or revelling party feel welcome. It used to be a cigar factory and today the space has been divided into an old-school bar complete with Delft Blue tiling on the walls and tables, a foliage-sheltered area outside in the alleyway and a sweet romantic restaurant. Ideal for the clandestine encounter.

SWING LOW SWEET CHARIOT

14 Suite

3 Sint Nicolaasstraat 43

Frank Traas and Rob Zorab were old hands on Amsterdam's bar circuit by the time they opened Suite in 2002, after their first venture, Diep Venue (p. 17), was such a success. It was the popularity of their bar on the Nieuwezijds Voorburgwal that led them to open the second: 'there was no room left in Diep for our friends'. Suite is furnished with an eclectic mix of flea-market finds and the guys are rightly proud of the retro result. Their own notoriety on the local scene ensured that this place was an immediate hit. But Traas and Zorab are not about flash-in-the-pan fashion. Suite does attract a butterfly crowd, but it is not pretentious. They serve a choice of French, Japanese and tapas dishes. There is also a huge pool table, which converts into a 22-seat dining table during meal shifts, and a dinner and after-dinner DJ in the house, as Traas loves music and also plays in the rough rock'n'roll band Heiland ('saviour').

COCKTAIL CULTURE

80 Madame Jeanette

21 1e Van Der Helststraat 42

Mention ID&T to any Dutch person and the first thing they think of is the 'gabber' (hard-core techno) music of the rave culture. This is because ID&T – the company run by Duncan Stutterheim – is responsible for some of the biggest parties that the Netherlands has ever known. Eight times a year 30,000 dancing Dutch people convene to party the night away under a spectacular light show to the beats of Marko V, Armin van Buren and a host of international rave DJs. Stutterheim hosted his first party, attended by over 10,000 punters, when he was 21 and hasn't looked back, but his activities over the years also reflect his own maturity. In 2000 he opened the fabulous people bar (and restaurant) Madame Jeanette with Ricardo Sporkslede and Bas Frenkel Frank. Sporkslede now runs the Fabulous Shaker Boys cocktail school for bartenders, so it is no surprise that Madame Jeanette prides itself on fancy drinks – and fanciable people.

48 **Bar ARC**

51 Reguliersdwarsstraat 44

Reguliersdwarsstraat is Amsterdam's 'gay street' and the bars and clubs that line it range from cruisy to…well, less cruisy. Not quite so ARC (abbreviation of Angelique Rob Company), who opened it as their first bar in 2002. Angelique Schippers and Rob de Jong are trying to appeal to a gay–straight mix and Rob estimates the breakdown to be 70:30 in the former's favour. They wanted glamour and good cocktails and thanks to the Fabulous Shaker Boys (the cocktail company who trained the bar staff) and the interior by Eric Kuster of B. Inc Interior Stuff, they have achieved both. Glass, leather and wenge wood provide the backdrop to the lights that can change colour, mirroring the mood of the bar and weather outside. With the addition of subdued reflective gold lacquer behind the bar and tables and an orange-gold broken laminate skin on a 15-by-6-metre wall, ARC is sultry, attracting a grown-up crowd who move on when they want to enjoy more than just drinks and the French International cuisine of this very democratic establishment.

48 Joia

40 Korte Leidsedwarsstraat 45

Joia (Joy Opens In Amsterdam) has the potential to mess with your mind as well as your kidneys. The owner, Casper Reijnders, commissioned this decadent cocktail lounge (and Cuban restaurant) from Eric Kuster at B. Inc Interior Stuff, having already worked with him on the restaurant NoA (Noodles of Amsterdam). Kuster's design company's name is colloquial Dutch for 'nice boy' and he, Erhan Borren and Eric Jonkers attempt to live up to their self-proclamation. Joia embodies conceptual art outside of the white cube. The predominant use of ruby is magnified tenfold with mirrors on the ceiling and walls; the addition of packaged bamboo in glass casing, 'à la Damien Hirst', forms the rear vista and effects sultry jungle sexiness transplanted into a brothel in 1930s Pigalle. Kuster found some sheep's horns and, with his textile training, moulded wall lamps to front the heavy velvet-textured, red damask paper. Although it is located along an alley off the tourist frenzy of the Leidseplein, Joia's glowing fervour seems to keep the less sophisticated drinkers at bay.

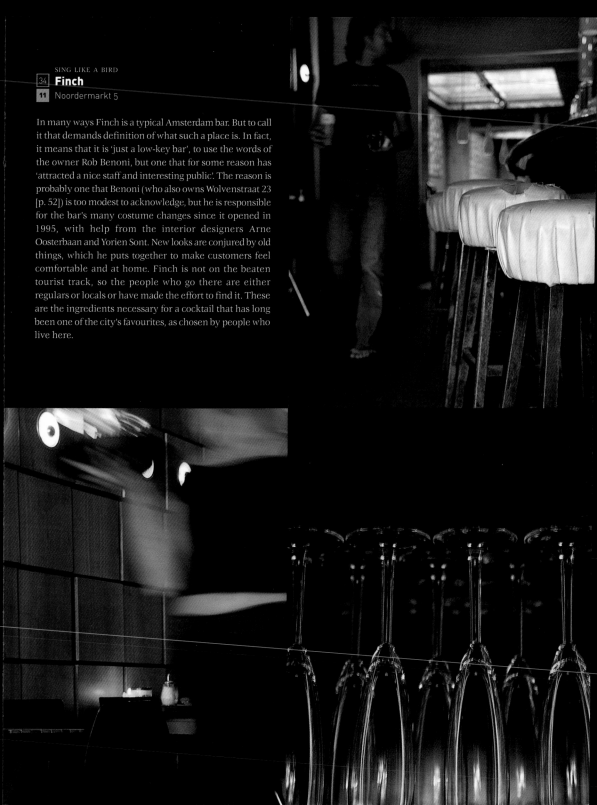

34 Finch

11 Noordermarkt 5

In many ways Finch is a typical Amsterdam bar. But to call it that demands definition of what such a place is. In fact, it means that it is 'just a low-key bar', to use the words of the owner Rob Benoni, but one that for some reason has 'attracted a nice staff and interesting public'. The reason is probably one that Benoni (who also owns Wolvenstraat 23 [p. 52]) is too modest to acknowledge, but he is responsible for the bar's many costume changes since it opened in 1995, with help from the interior designers Arne Oosterbaan and Yorien Sont. New looks are conjured by old things, which he puts together to make customers feel comfortable and at home. Finch is not on the beaten tourist track, so the people who go there are either regulars or locals or have made the effort to find it. These are the ingredients necessary for a cocktail that has long been one of the city's favourites, as chosen by people who live here.

Wouter Brev and Christian Vos were the driving force behind the transformation of this former harbour generator building into a glamorous nightclub, dance studio and restaurant. When they acquired the space in 2001 it was derelict, strewn with garbage and birds' nests. But thanks to the architects Ruud van Empel and VASD, it has been renovated and divided into three main areas: a 140-seat restaurant, a dance floor and champagne bar. The restaurant is perforated by natural light, and minimal wagon-wheel-shaped chandeliers provide further illumination. It overlooks a terrace where more seating is provided and a playful touch added in the form of boules. Inside the club tables are set around the stage and the glamour of bygone eras is recreated through plush reds in a golden champagne bar. Post dining, the chairs and tables are removed and the whole of Panama become a fantastic dance venue.

The team that run the Supperclub (p. 151) – Bert van der Leden's IQ Creative – have most recently drawn inspiration from Arabian mystique and opened this lounge, bar and restaurant with a Middle-Eastern vibe. What both venues do well is present total concept. Guests first dine, then dance and finally relax. They never have to leave the venue to have three different experiences. Once your imagination has been captured, you are sold the CD and can continue the groove in your own home. Once again, the design architects Gilian Schrofor and Rob Wagamans of Concrete have worked their magic and created a sublime interior. Almost floor-level cushioned seating and hanging linen curtains recreate the Bedouin tents of the desert where sharing plates of meze and drinking tea from tiny glasses is de rigueur hospitality. The staff uniforms are by Aziz, kilims by Barbara Broekman and food by the Lebanese chef Ali Ballout. On ground level, Nomads sits above its sister club, More, which is located in the basement.

STRANGERS IN THE NIGHT

14 **Supperclub**

2 Jonge Roelensteeg 21

First you have to find the Supperclub, and then you have
to get in. But once these problems have been dealt with (it
is hidden up an alleyway and booking ahead ensures
entry) an astounding evening is guaranteed. The world's
first concept club was the brainwave of Suzanne Oxenaar,
Thor Vos and Guda Sloop. Vos and Sloop now run a hotel
in Barcelona and Oxenaar is behind the Lloyd Hotel (p. 96),
but the Supperclub's international renown has evolved
without them, thanks to the intervention of Bert van der
Leden, who turned the club into a multinational brand.
Entrance is via an imposing wooden door and a marble
staircase leads up to a three-storey-high white room whose
walls are flanked by white lounge beds. Diners recline
on these and are entertained by waif-like transvestites. The
room has an energetic ultra-violet edge and is supremely
sexy. Once the show is over, guests move to the sultry
red disco downstairs. The enigmatic interior bears the
hallmark of its creators, Gilian Schrofor and Rob Wagamans
of Concrete.

shop

Amsterdam boasts over 10,000 shops, 141 galleries, 165 antique boutiques and 26 markets, making it a clear leader as the largest shopping centre in the country. The novelty of shopping here relies on the educated eye of the store owner, whose creativity can intertwine themes and products, which results in a gallery-style environment featuring the 'best of' shoes, Dutch designers, furniture, coffee and even toothbrushes. Simple tangible goods like olive oil are the starting point for an exploration of every type, colour, style, scent and accessory, leaving the customer enriched both sensually and intellectually by all the possibilities on offer.

Droog & Co is the home of Droog Design, founded by Gijs Bakker and Renny Ramakers in 1993. Droog's mission statement is 'to make a contribution to international debate about design through projects, exhibitions, workshops and publications.' They have consistently achieved this and are renowned in the design arena for initiating and developing experimental projects. They were behind Jurgen Bij's streetscape project in Tokyo and the knotted chair of Marcel Wanders. The reputation of Droog has put them in a position to nurture young design talent by inviting graduates to take part in the commissions they receive from international firms and institutions. Over the years, these have included working with design studios such as Concrete (which created Supperclub [p. 151], and Blender [p. 125]), Flex in Delft and United Statements of Rotterdam. Their work is simple, witty, clever and practical: recent designs include bubblewrap-inspired glasses and opaque plastic blob shapes to stick on windows to make them less transparent.

A sense of peace descends the moment you enter the world of Pilat & Pilat. The furniture, the colours, the light, the way the 800-square-metre corner store is laid out all come together to create an almost ecclesiastical calm. The interior design business bears the name of the founder, Gjalt Pilat, and his daughter, Kristien. They are based in their native Friesland in the north of Holland where they run another showroom and Gjalt's latest project in the form of a new hotel, Herberg de Waard van Ternaard (p. 182). The embodiment of silence in furniture is no accident: *rust en eenvoud* ('calm and simplicity') is the unofficial company slogan. It is attained in heavy pieces of oak or walnut, crafted into tables with no apparent joins and in sofas whose wood base is softened with the addition of deep red or brown cushioned fabrics. Benches mimic the tables and replace chairs as monastic levellers. Although they predominantly sell their own line, lamps by Margot Nije and other Dutch designers complement the Pilat & Pilat ethic.

The De Ridder name has been synonymous with quality rattan and wicker furniture since this showroom and workshop was founded in 1896 by the current owner's grandfather, P.F.L. De Ridder. For over 40 years he supplied furniture for ships and was the specialist designer of first-class interiors on the Holland-Amerika Lijn. Now at the helm of the family business, Frits De Ridder works with his wife, Louise, and their two children, Joost and Justine, on a site that spans the ground floor of three town houses. He has responded to contemporary design by also including wood, stainless steel and fabrics. To underline his belief that: 'in the last five years Dutch design has reached a level of independent creative expression that is matched by a progressive business acumen', he commissioned Piet Hein Eek to produce a collection in Javan teak scrap wood. De Ridder also supports emerging talent, such as Monique Burger, offering development assistance and show space for today's ideas realized as tomorrow's classics.

Although primarily a shop, the relationship between the founder, Dick Dankers, and his partner, Cok de Rooy, with the furniture and industrial designers has produced a dynamic collection since its formation in 1985. With 625 square metres of space, The Frozen Fountain maximizes the potential of designers by staging exhibitions that are often produced in association with other reputable institutions, such as the Mondriaan Foundation. The tremendous enthusiasm created by interdisciplinary shows raised the profile of all involved and Dankers saw the potential for providing the public and designers with an unequalled opportunity to explore and present work. The access to Dutch talent and its success in the international arena led to the formation of the Dutch Individuals Foundation, which Dankers and De Rooy use to assist young designers into the industry. Armed with their achievements and success, they have most recently started an on-site Textile Museum, providing the only looms in Europe still to weave original pure linen damask.

Since 1998, the Pakhuis Amsterdam has provided 4,500 square metres of exhibition space profiling eye-candy for design aficionados from all over the world. The building began life as the Asia cocoa warehouse at the turn of the 19th century and an industrial use of the space is still apparent in the exposed cast-iron pillars, girders and wooden beams that support the structure. But there is more to this design Mecca than meets the eye. Part of it pays homage to contemporary creation and creators; part offers commercial convenience for consumers. Information is given on where to buy the items that fall under the gallery remit. Pakhuis Amsterdam is critically acclaimed for combining the gallery-store concept. Curvaceous chairs with complementary lights by Louis Poulson and Meubelindustrie Gelderland's full-sized sofa-seats-for-one provide a start for an education in predominantly Dutch, but also international design. A restaurant on the upper level breaks out of the building in a two-storey glass appendage.

American-born, Dutch-married Hann combines an assortment of dinnerware, cutlery and glassware from the finest suppliers in the world with handmade ceramics from local Dutch artists. The shop's small interior is typical of her appreciation for contrasting styles and materials. She sets out a 1967 stainless-steel coffeepot beside mother-of-pearl spoons and porcelain crockery to emphasize what she calls 'their sense of right'. Major brands such as Artoria, Royal Copenhagen, Orrefors, Georg Jensen, Rosenthal and Stelton have captured her imagination and she has found a place to arrange them 'correctly' in the overall look of the store. Two of her personal favourites are the beautiful porcelain cups by Dutch JAS/MV and a perfectly balanced stirring spoon by C. Hugo Pott. Margot Nije reveals her wit in the lipstick imprint that she has glazed on to the rim of her inventive ceramic beakers.

Simon de Jong and Stefan Reiters met whilst working at the antiquarian bookstore Kok in Amsterdam. Just out of university, they were keen to learn about the dusty world of the second-hand book trade. A shared creative instinct, an aversion to dust and a desire to make the act of buying books an event drove them from their alma mater to set up shop across town. JOOT (standing for Just Out Of Time – which is the common factor of the 'nearly new' books they sell) was born in 2001 and its distinctive full-metal façade is from the Michel de Klerk Amsterdam school of architecture. They call their 'bookery' the 'first kinky antiquarian bookshop ever' and it is indeed the antithesis of a traditional second-hand store, with wide open space, light colours, industrial metallic cases and leaded glass maintaining a fresh feel. A strong selection of bibliophile editions, literature, art, photography and philosophy books combines with original art from the changing exhibitions mounted in the gallery space.

WHY DON'T YOU?

48 **Young Designers United**

41 Keizersgracht 447

For a such a design-conscious city it is incredible that it took a *buitenlander* (foreigner) to provide a long-overdue platform for young fashion design talent in Amsterdam. Polish-born Angelika Wasyleski opened her store in 2003 and operates it in effect as a collective. She contacted fashion academy tutors and friends in the fashion world and offered to rent rail space to designers who wanted to get their work in the public domain. YDU is located in a prime retail area and overheads are high, so the designers share the rent but receive 80 per cent of the sale price for their garments. At any one time there are several designers in the store, meaning that customers are going to have a very wide choice of styles. Xuan-Thu Nguyen is one of her most talented protégés. His geometric suits for women have delicate and fragile accents of colour and they are smart and mature. Amber Rose is a different story; she creates sexy streetwise clothes for girls. Natasja Fakkeldij is a milliner of extravagant hats. No doubt some of these names will go global.

FLORISTRY FANTASY

70 **Menno Kroon**

6 Cornelis Schuytstraat 11

Menno Kroon was a freelance florist for about three years before opening his shop some 12 years ago. He adopts a novel approach to flower arranging and one that has seen his work and reputation travel far across the Netherlands. At the crack of dawn he and his team of ten florists travel to the famous flower auctions at Aalsmeer and Vleuten and buy up their daily selection. Four times a year Kroon reinvents the look of his shop and celebrates this with an opening. In 2003 he commissioned Walther van Ekkendonk to paint parrots on the walls; the florists then created bouquets using only the vibrant colours of the birds. This was followed by an aptly autumnal theme of Black Magic. Yet, whatever the season, the decadent abundance of exotics such as Lady's Slipper orchids, protea flowers, ginger, mascari and heliconia is breathtaking. And with such pungent aromas, breathing can be rather heady.

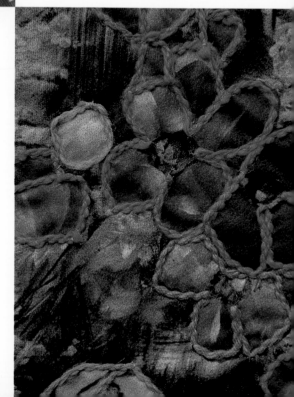

Van Ravenstein is a one-stop shop for Belgian fashion design in the Netherlands. Although Dutch herself, Gerda van Ravenstein's affinity for the famous Antwerp Six fashion designers of the 1990s means pieces from most collections are present and accounted for. However, Dries van Noten, Ann Demeulemeester and Dirk Bikkembergs are the only remaining designers from the original six. The next generation has arrived in the form of A.F. Vandevorst, Bernhard Willhelm and Veronique Branquinho, and she is the only Dutch outlet for Viktor + Rolf. The common denominator of these designers is practical design with functional tailoring in wearable sizes. This style's popularity in the Netherlands can be attributed to its appeal to tall Dutch women who get around on bicycles. Of course it is the impeccable tailoring methods, based on deconstruction techniques, that have kept some of these names at the forefront of international fashion for more than a decade.

I WANNA WALK LIKE YOU

70 **Shoebaloo**

4 P.C. Hooftstraat 80

Shoebaloo has come a long way since Hartog A. Streim opened as a boot retailer in the Jordaan in 1975. He currently presides over five shops in the Netherlands and is the self-confessed eccentric product of two Jewish cobbler families. As well as his own line, Streim is perhaps better known as the ultimate buyer in the country for Gucci, Prada, Dolce & Gabbana and Yves Saint Laurent footwear. His own creativity is best exemplified in the design of his outlets, and nowhere more so than in the most recent facelift (2003) by the architects Meyer en Van Schooten at this branch. Extreme futurism and organic structure are combined in a space that appears as a homage to a 22nd-century spaceship. The display shelving glows green, rose or amber, and the reflective rear wall and floor create an illusion of deeper space in the 80-square-metre store. Ultra-white pod seating and a control panel (for trying on and paying for the shoes) are pragmatic reminders of the space's original function.

Warmer is to boots what Blahník is to the strappy slingback. Paul and Renée married some 30 years ago (she wore gold shoes) and, sharing a taste for fashion, developed a clothing line. Fifteen years ago they narrowed the remit to footwear and have been making shoes that lead seasonal trends ever since. 'Some of our clients phone us up to ask what clothes they should buy each season,' commented Renée, 'as they know that their fashion choices will be dictated by what they are wearing on their feet. And that will be down to the designs of Paul and myself.' This may sound unorthodox, but a visit to a Paul Warmer shop (there are now three in Holland) reveals why. They craft boots of astounding proportion and have a fearless attitude to colour and form. Flat, pointed boots retain the edge of high fashion, but are supremely functional too. They combine stretch elastic with soft leather to hold calf shape and mould the boot top right over the knee. Heeled varieties have been made in glittering silver à la *Barbarella* and more recently in acid neon pinks, orange and green. It is not surprising that Benelux stylists look to their shop for ideas, as their window displays also tell current fashion tales.

48 **Analik**

12 Hartenstraat 36

The concept of Analik as an independent Dutch fashion label was recently extended when Analik Brouwer opened up a gallery store, aptly named Next Door, in the space beside the shop from which she has sold her quirky clothing since 1998. A 1996 graduate of Utrecht's design and art academy, Analik initially started commercial design in London with a collection for the Sign of the Times label. Back in the Netherlands, her work has always been warmly received by the fashion media and has featured in German and American *Vogue*, Japanese *Elle* and British *i-D*. The strength of her work lies in the cut and shape of the clothing, and she has experimented with form by using harder textiles. Of course, every season is different, but she is integral to Amsterdam's small (but growing) fashion face. Her project Next Door will see her fulfil the role of curator for emerging European artists and designers. The rest of the building has been renovated as a two-room, one-suite B&B, where everything in the rooms will be for sale.

70 **Possen.com**

19 Van Baerlestraat 39

Possen.com is a revolution against traditional, widespread preconceptions associated with buying made-to-measure garments. Without any physical contact, a customer's body size is measured using body scan technology that processes the information and displays it on a screen in the form of a 'DigiTwin'. The owners Bas Possen and Diederik de Flines claim that the accuracy of digitally measuring the body guarantees a perfect fit and disregards the necessity for trying on more than one suit or for repeat fittings. The technological approach is applicable for a range of suits, jackets, overcoats and skirts. Once scanned, the customer chooses the fabric and cut of the garment and all this information is sent to ateliers in Germany and Italy then returned, to the specification of their owner, four weeks later. The system has the potential to save future fitting times and is the stuff of science fiction dreams, realized in cut apparel 'in your size only'.

80 Gassan Diamonds

23 Nieuwe Uilenburgerstraat 173–75

In ancient Greece diamonds were believed to be slivers of stars fallen from the sky, and their international history as objects of lust has several scenes set in Amsterdam. In 1880 the Boas brothers' diamond factory was the largest of its technological kind in the whole of Europe. The three brothers purchased rough stones in London, polished them in Amsterdam and sold them in Paris. With the German occupation the Boas family fled the country and never really returned to take up the diamond reins in the same way again. Three of their colleagues were killed in concentration camps and the factory was liquidated in 1944. But in 1990 it was acquired by the grandsons of Samuel Gassan, who himself had founded a diamond business in 1945. The architect Ed Veerendaal has re-created the Emerald City as its interior, an aptly imposing and stark environment in which to buy precious stones. Gassan offers free 90-minute daily tours as an opportunity to witness the diamond polishing and setting process and a glimpse into the private world of international diamond dealing.

CIGAR CITY

14 PGC Hajenius

43 Rokin 92–96

Pantaleon Gerhard Coenraad Hajenius founded his cigar shop in 1826. It moved to its current humidity-controlled location in 1915. The Art Déco interior is a national monument featuring oak-panelled walls and a richly decorated ceiling, as well as the largest cigar library in Europe. It sells the exclusive three lines of Hajenius cigars: the Sumatra selection (lighter, the morning smoke), the Grand Finale range (which blends tobacco from Sumatra, Havana and Brazil as the after-dinner smoke of choice) and the HBPR (hand-bunched-pressed-rolled cigar that is specially made to a traditional method in Nicaragua). The shop houses private humidors and couriers supplies to the owners when their personal stock runs low. Cigar courses are run for novices and cigars can be enjoyed on-site with a tea or coffee.

In recent years, oils have become a thoughtful alternative to wine as gifts for dinner-party hosts. Manfred Meeuwig was hip to this fact and to the potential and prolific choice of oils, having spent several years as a chef working in Paris and later as a food stylist, a job that remains the focus of his time. He opened Meeuwig & Zn (abbreviation of 'sons') in 1995, installing raw wooden floors and shelves in the space. Stainless-steel tankards of oil line the walls above the zinc counter. The selection is an education in oils: the nutty pumpkin seed from Austria, lemongrass oil, his own brand of lemon and basil or rare almond oil from Morocco. Dutch mustards from Zwolle or the renowned old factory in Doesburg, Zeeland, come in dill, honey and garlic blends. Meeuwig also stocks vinegars, and a favourite is made by a friend, Walter Abma, in the north of Holland. The vinegar bases come from seasonal ingredients: the winter months produce fruity tangs and the summer red basil, mint, tarragon and fennel.

The antique façade, age-darkened woods and peaceful atmosphere at Wijs & Zonen provide the initial clue that this coffee-and-tea specialist dates back to 1828. The coffee bean arrived in Holland in the mid-17th century via the VOC (Dutch East India Company), when ships sailed right up the Amstel River to dock and deposit their loads directly at the shop. The Dutch discovered a taste for coffee and today they serve and drink it as other nations do water. Free cups of freshly filtered coffee are available in many supermarkets, and it is considered reasonable behaviour for employees to refuse to start work unless the company's percolator is wafting that distinctive aroma. Wijs & Zonen offer over 20 varieties, some with unusual origins in Cuba, Hawaii and Yemen. Tea is an equally popular beverage and here there are over 120 blends, many made from the traditional recipes of yesteryear. Their 'afternoon blend' is a secret mix of five teas whose smoky tones reveal Lapsang Souchong and Darjeeling as two ingredients. The others remain a beguiling mystery.

CHOCOLATE OPERA

14 **Puccini Bomboni**

13 Staalstraat 17

Over a decade ago Ans van Soelen opened a dessert shop selling cakes, candies and chocolates. The chocolates outsold the other confectionery and Van Soelen narrowed her scope, but not her selection. She sells enormous, divine chocolates from a contemporary glass store not far from the Amsterdam opera house (hence the inspiration for naming the shop after the Italian composer). Her chocolates are made on-site from all natural ingredients and are unique in local chocolate culture as she refrains from using sugar, fondant or butter in any of her recipes. However, Van Soelen is not afraid to experiment with flavour and lemongrass, thyme, rhubarb, nutmeg, pepper and vanilla pod with poppy-seed have all been infused into her plain, milk and white varieties. Part of the concoction process can be witnessed through a glass façade to the side of the shop, which allows an enticing peak into the delectable world of chocolate couture.

34 Unlimited Delicious

20 Haarlemmerstraat 122

Kees Raat grew up working in the family patisserie, which already spans six generations. He started making chocolates and supplying hotels and restaurants across the Netherlands in 1990 and finally opened his own shop in 2001. He has decorated it like the inside of a sumptuous box of chocolates: glittering silver mirrors and sparkling gold paper adorn the walls. His sense of humour is allowed free rein in self-styled advertising posters featuring women literally dressed in Raat's home-made chocolate paste (watch out for new poster campaigns). He sells divine hot *puur* ('dark') chocolate cups distilled from cocoa beans with the minerals retained, which coat the throat when sipped. Chocolates are made using traditional methods but with a contemporary twist, and flavours include cardamom, jasmine tea and saki. Most recently, Raat has developed a line of ice creams: real orange with Campari, panacotta and orange caramel brownie.

70 De Waterwinkel

20 Roelof Hartstraat 10

De Waterwinkel is to H_2O what a connoisseur's cellar is to wine. You could be forgiven for mistaking its arced entrance, wooden floors, Roman friezes and shelves stocked with bottles for a specialist wine supplier. But John Willem Bakker's shop sells only 'the clear stuff', and every variety of it. There is bottled water from almost every country that produces it, Greece, Italy and as far afield as Australia. More local sources are represented by Barleduk, from Utrecht, and Sourcy, which is bottled in Breda. The atmosphere in the store is conducive to medicinal relief and the sound of a waterfall is the backdrop to water selection. The popularity of flavoured mixtures, spring-sourced and mineral varieties that calm the heart and ease the stomach has recently been surpassed by oxygen-infused water that claims to diffuse hangovers and impart vitality fast, as its properties ensure swift system assimilation.

When this distillery opened in 1679 it was normal to have a tasting room where testing (and enjoying) could take place. Wynand Fockink took over in 1730 and the name remained even though the tasting house was bought by Dutch liquor distillers Bols in 1955. Entrance is via a narrow alleyway situated at the back of the Krasnapolsky Hotel on the Dam square. The main tasting room looks as if it has not changed since the 17th century: there is no music, gambling machines or entertainment, no tables or chairs. The focus is the booze. There are spitting troughs built into a low wooden bar and the shelves bend under the weight of heavy liquor (as do some of the customers after a few 'tastings'). Wynand Fockink offer 20 different *jenevers* and 50 old Dutch liquors, all brewed under the house label. They further mix the drinks on-site, resulting in popular favourites such as the berry-flavoured Boswandeling. The *jenever* has many guises here: flavoured with coriander, aniseed or herbs, or sweetened with caramel and ripened in wooden vats.

Enter past a back-lit wall featuring what to most is the alien language of the periodic table, through sliding doors into a circular space sporting a glowing verdant carpet of ginkgo biloba with walls of aquamarine cabinets stocked with herbal and conventional cures for whatever ails you. This is Concrete's vision for a modern apothecary as prescribed by the pharmacist owner, Marjan Terpstra. With a body of work more synonymous with nightclubs and fashion boutiques, Concrete's approach to designing a pharmacy was not hindered by bland preconception.

This 'blind vision' has resulted in an extraordinary, multifunctional, expanding educational environment. There is a glass reading room in which to learn about alternative therapies, free computer access to examine illnesses and drugs and a Perspex box for depositing old drugs so they can be disposed of ecologically by the professionals that run this place. For Lairesse Apotheek is no alternative therapy retailer; it is a professional, functioning pharmacy. Pensioners are more prevalent in here than design aficionados. Concrete had to cope with practical restrictions dictated by pharmacists who need chemicals to be situated in premeditated locations. Their solution is proof that conventional activity may be enhanced by subtly discerning design.

retreat

Structured urban planning across the Netherlands and a reliable train service ensure that you are rarely aware that this is the most densely populated country in Europe, as well as one of the smallest. In the space of an hour you can be contemplating culture on the Museumplein and partying Ibiza-style on a (weather permitting) sun-drenched beach. The rural Holland of clogs and windmills exists, but in it there are sumptuous day spas, elegant micro-hotels, windswept sand dunes and the oldest woods in Europe. Six retreats have been chosen for their distinctive character, but all are fantasy-fulfilling, romantic refuges.

Apeldoorn: The Green Heart

- Paleis Het Loo
- Kröller-Müller Museum
- De Havixhorst
- De Librije

Less than 100 kilometres (60 miles) east of Amsterdam (about an hour by train from Centraal Station) gnarly trees break through the soil and woods cover the earth for miles. It is perhaps a scene more associated with the centre of the Continent. But these woods are the oldest in Europe and were once the hunting ground of royal families who would travel to the scattered lodges for blood sport. The Green Heart of the Netherlands lies in the 20,000-hectare (50,000-acre) Hoge Veluwe National Park. The city of Apeldoorn sits just east of these trees, close to Holland's answer to Versailles, the Paleis Het Loo (Palace of the Woods), whose Dutch-Baroque rooms and formal French gardens are now open to the public. De Hoge Veluwe was once the private property of the Kröller-Müller family, but they gave it to the nation along with an art collection that is now the third most important in the country: 285 pieces by Van Gogh and the largest open-air gallery in Europe with work by Serra, Rodin, Oldenburg, Hepworth and Giacometti on display at their namesake museum. The woodlands vary from thick forest to open rolling veld and they are still inhabited by boars, roe deer, red deer and a rich bird life.

Around 57 kilometres (35 miles) northwards lies the fiercely religious town of Staphorst, but on its outskirts is a bolt-hole whose resplendence is a modern-day match for the lodges of yore. Château de Havixhorst was once the premier residence in all of Drenthe and home of the aristocratic family De Vos van Steenwijk. Jos Wijland and his wife, Karin Klinkenberg, have transformed it into a softly furnished eight-suite villa of style, with Klinkenberg worshipping at the altars of Designer's Guild, Timney Fowler and Mercure. Their restaurant presents an alternative to Jonnie Boer's De Librije in nearby Zwolle, although his place is reputed to be the best restaurant in the Netherlands.

Rotterdam: Architecture Mecca

- Nederlands Architectuur Instituut
- Kunsthal
- Boijmans Van Beuningen museum
- Kijk-Kubus
- Hotel New York

Rotterdam is in a state of flux. As a busy, industrial port city, perhaps it has always been like that, but never more so than over the past 60 years, as it rose like a phoenix from the ashes after the ten-minute German aerial bombing on 14 May 1940, which razed almost 30,000 buildings over 257 hectares (635 acres). It was this flattened empty canvas in the centre that was responsible for Rotterdam's lack of resemblance to any other city in the Netherlands. Gone are the twee canal bridges and cobbled streets. They have been replaced by fierce young architecture that claws skyward, defying gravity and reinventing the profession as an experimental study. Architects from all over the world made inspirational pilgrimages to Rotterdam. No wonder the Nederlands Architectuur Instituut is located here; it flanks one end of the Museumpark, which is shared with (Rotterdam's darling) Rem Koolhaas's Kunsthal, the Natuurmuseum and the Boijmans Van Beuningen museum. Inevitably, the centre is now considered an outdated homage to the 1950s and controversy has arisen between traditionalists who think it should be left untouched and younger thinkers who want it replaced. Full appreciation of the state of play is best witnessed by taking a water taxi from the northern abutment of Ben van Berkel's iconic Erasmus Bridge, the world's largest bascule bridge. On the five-minute crossing to the Kop van Zuid peninsula look at Renzo Piano's KPN Telecom Tower and back to the Witte Huis, which at 45 metres was Europe's first skyscraper in 1898. Glimpse Piet Bloom's 1984 housing juxtaposition, realized as the Kijk-Kubus. The south side of the Nieuwe Maas is where the principal redevelopment is taking place. Old warehouses are being turned into new cafés: Café Rotterdam's balcony affords incredible views, as does the terrace of the Hotel New York, which dominates the end of this dock peninsula and was once the offices of the Holland-Amerika Lijn.

GARDEN ESCAPE

Haarlem and Bloemendaal: Haute Grandeur and Ibiza-style Beach Madness

- Spaarne 8
- Park Tower Suite
- Duinlust Vitality Resort
- De Tropen aan Zee

At only 20 kilometres (12 miles) from Amsterdam (about 15 minutes by train), Haarlem is practically a suburb of the capital. The city skyline is dominated by the 14th-century Grote Kerk, an indication of the church's financial influence during that period. As a drive through the tree-lined, mansion-flanked roads of nearby Heemstede and Overveen will reveal, Haarlem is the epicentre of the most affluent neighbourhoods in the country.

In its centre, wrapped by the Teylers Museum, stands a town house with an ordinary façade that hides a supremely elegant micro-hotel named after its address: Spaarne 8. Janneke and Peter Schoenmaker decorated a wing of their home and transformed it into two suites so sumptuous that they rate right off the five-star hotel scale. Both rooms have terraces in the garden designed by Dick Beijer (who was also responsible for the outdoors of homes belonging to Sirs Elton John and Terence Conran), which allow contemplation of the oldest tree in Haarlem. Spaarne 8 proved such an inspirational design for boutique hotels that regular guests, the van Schootens, opened their own version across town. The divine rooms (living + dining + bathroom) of the unique Park Tower Suite were decorated by Janneke and also lead onto a garden by Beijer.

In nearby Overveen, another mansion estate was recently given new life by Annemarie Hemken who transformed it into the Duinlust Vitality Resort. The complex comprises über-modern workout facilities, hammam, treatment rooms, a state-of-the-art health-food bar, a centre for integrative medicine and a Downtown lounge set in lush grounds. The day spa is an oasis of meditative calm providing motivation to achieve the body beautiful via massage, meditation and muscle-inducing cardiovascular graft. The architect Amiran Simhy reflected the inner beauty and peace that the sanctuary aims to achieve for its patrons in his own use of a vivacious palette, contrasted with natural stone.

Just 5 kilometres (3 miles) away, Bloemendaal is the destination beach for hip Amsterdammers who descend every weekend in the summer to whoop it up in 'clubs' that are erected on the beach from March through November. The summer scene is a breathtaking sea of bikinied bodies and surfing boys who sleep on the sun-kissed sand and dance on the decks of Bloomingdale (ID&T, Duncan Stutterheim's summer palace), Woodstock (hippy vibe complete with hammocks and cushions scattered on the sand and impromptu yoga classes held in between DJ shifts) and République (slightly more glam body-conscious crowd). Each of the Ibiza-style 'clubs' provides bars, lounges, food and a different style of music and décor, where locals kick back and enjoy the summertime vibe of their choice. The spectacle is overlooked by the all-year-round restaurant De Tropen aan Zee, so even winter visitors can watch the glowing sun descend into the North Sea, often accompanied by a round of applause from any Dutch people present.

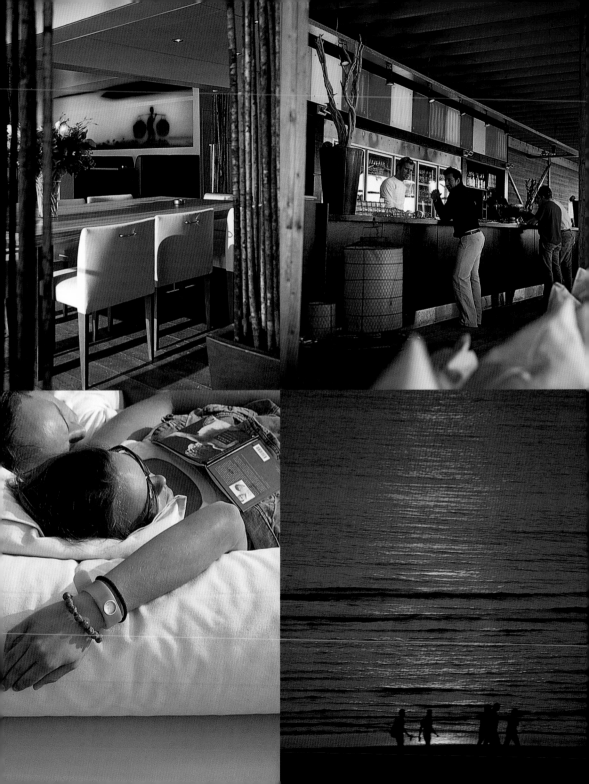

Leiden: Student City

- De Beukenhof
- Hortus Botanicus
- De Burcht

Leiden's repute is based on several facts that any 'Nederlander' will recite if asked. It is the birthplace of three of the nation's most celebrated painters: Rembrandt, Jan van Goyen and Jan Havicksz Steen. The home of the Pilgrim Fathers between 1609 and 1620, it also houses the first university of the country, founded in 1581, which transforms an otherwise quiet city into one continuously infused with the refreshing vitality of new people, new ideas, new culture and some ancient museums. From Amsterdam it can be reached in about half an hour.

Just west of Leiden is De Beukenhof hotel and restaurant, taken over by Erwin Rozendal and Jacky Webber in 1996. Already established across the Netherlands for its cuisine, De Beukenhof (The Beech Tree Garden) lists Elizabeth Taylor, Maria Callas and Queen Beatrix amongst its patrons of the past half-century. Webber remodelled the suites as nine high-design-influenced rooms, which feature slim televisions in the bathrooms and private saunas. She artfully contrasted contemporary glass, furniture and fixtures with the history of the 300-year-old building. It is now a member of the 'small luxury hotels of the world'.

Back in the centre, the educational complex is spread across the canal-ridden city. One of the most celebrated faculties houses the Hortus Botanicus (botanical gardens). A new three-storey glasshouse provides vertigo-inducing views of rare species of cacti and palm trees from a metal grid walkway suspended from the ceiling of the transparent structure. There are steamy butterfly-filled hothouses and cool, minimal Japanese gardens. The first tulip bulb in Holland was bedded here and its introduction into Dutch soil was to become a crucial factor in the nation's fluctuating finances for generations to come.

The city's heart comprises little souk-like streets around the dominant St Pieterkerk, which hide boutiques and cafés. De Burcht (the fort) is a beautiful Art Déco bar with live jazz and an aquamarine, fresco-style ceiling. As its name suggests, it sits at the foot of the crumbling Leiden fortifications.

Noordwijk: Beside the Seaside, Beside the Sea

- Villa de Duinen
- Huize van Wely
- Hotels van Oranje

The western stretch of Dutch coastline running the length of the country is flanked by rolling dunes that protect this lowland from flooding. Meandering cycle-paths weave through the sandgrasses and connect the many little ocean-view towns. Although the beaches are consistently wide, sandy and windswept, each has a character reflective of the people who live close by. This ranges from gay-nude near Den Haag to Ibiza-club chaos at Bloemendaal and the family-friendly Wassanaar. As the crow flies, Amsterdam to Noordwijk is about 35 kilometres (22 miles) and leads a route through the bulb plantations so resplendent in the spring. Hotels line the promenade facing the Noordzee, as if to mirror the sun worshippers who flock to the water from May through October.

Set slightly back from the beach, Villa de Duinen is a quiet hotel and stylish restaurant conceived by Erik van Roon and Anne-Marie van der Plas. They recently restored the hotel to its former glory as a period *pension* or boarding house originally built in 1902. Each of the nine rooms is unique, but all draw inspiration from the earth tones of the surrounding dunes: custom-woven matting in storm-sea and terrace chairs in royal sky blue. The couple are equally passionate about food and their proximity to the sea enhances a menu rich in sea-farmed foods. As locals, they are proud to count the 'By Royal Appointment' Huize van Wely chocolatiers among their regular patrons and neighbours.

Dominating the tourist strip drag are the opulent Hotels van Oranje (the four-star Beach Hotel and the five-star Hotel Oranje in one complex), where Dutch financial whizz Harry Mens's TV show *Business Class* is filmed and pictures of Dutch royalty peer from every wall. The owners Bram Mol and Charles de Boer's flair for the ostentatious is spectacularly played out in their olympic-sized indoor pool (with wave machine) and sauna where Greek statues and a water garden are enjoyed by the naked patrons. Perhaps its most camp secret is the nude swimming from 6 pm every Friday, Saturday and Sunday evening.

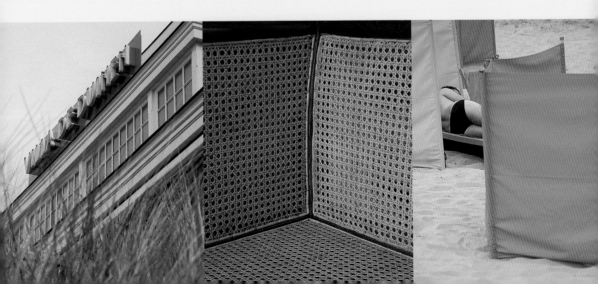

De Waddenzee: Low Land Big Sky
• Herberg de Waard van Ternaard

The state of Montana, USA, is referred to as big sky country but this subtitle is better applied to the lowlands of Holland, and nowhere more so than the northern region of Friesland, which lies some 130 kilometres (80 miles) north of Amsterdam. Stand on a roadside, gaze across green pastures and 80 per cent of your field of vision will be filled by blue-grey sky reflecting the eerie Dutch light, which has been captured and made familiar by the likes of Rembrandt and Vermeer. The farmland vista is broken only by windmills, cows and cycle paths, protected by the dykes (at 30 kilometres [18 miles] in length, the Afsluitdijk is the most impressive) that face across the Waddenzee to the archipelago of islands flanking Friesland and creating its own fishing pond, while forming a buffer against the North Sea beyond.

It is no surprise that this is the homeland of Gjalt Pilat, the furniture-designing craftsman who has been called 'the Armani of the North'. His sober use of oak and walnut carries an inherent sense of peace, which he markets with the unofficial company slogan *rust en eenvoud,* or 'calm and simplicity' (see Pilat & Pilat [p. 155]). His reputation brought him patronage from government consultant Garmt Visser some 15 years ago and their families became friends. In 2001 they decided to combine their skills and open a boutique hotel: Herberg de Waard van Ternaard, 'The Coach Inn of the Host of Ternaard'. Ternaard happens to be a tiny village in the north of the province, connected to the town of Leeuwarden (Friesland's capital and the birthplace of Escher and Mata Hari) by a bus that runs only once every two hours. It took them over a year to rebuild what had for a long time been the village watering hole, and Pilat's unique touch transformed it entirely, resulting in the award for 'Best Small Hotel of Holland', as selected by the prestigious *Reizen* magazine.

No two of the five first-floor slumber chambers are the same, although all subscribe to the slogan. Each is large enough to provide a sitting area that feels separate to the bed, where simple monotone sheets take the heat out of any colour provided by the sofa cushions. As in his Amsterdam showroom, Pilat & Pilat, Gjalt's own creations are complemented by the creations of Margot Nije, whose oversized lamps leave the ceiling on a cord and hang close to the floor, defining controlled puddles of illumination when lit. The ground level is divided between a lounge with bar (which doubles as an impromptu office for Visser), a decked terrace out front, a smashed-shell-smattered garden and the restaurant, which is rapidly developing a destination reputation in its own right. The chef Marielle Swarte bakes her own bread and uses local suppliers for the fresh fish, fruit, vegetables and dairy products (think Friesian cows), for which the region is celebrated. Visser is turning the Town House opposite into an artist's residence, which will further Ternaard as the aesthetic asylum of the north.

contact

All telephone numbers are given for dialling locally: the country code for the Netherlands is 31; the city code for Amsterdam is 020. Calling from abroad, one dials (+31 20) plus the number given below. Telephone numbers in the retreat section are given for dialling from Amsterdam: if calling from abroad, dial the country code (31) and drop the 0 in the number. The number in brackets by the name is the page number on which the entry appears.

A. Boeken [18]
Nieuwe Hoogstraat 31
1011 HD Amsterdam
T/F 626 7205
E   ar.boeken@wxs.nl
W   www.aboeken.nl

Absinthe [17]
Nieuwezijds Voorburgwal 171
1012 RK Amsterdam
T   320 6780
F   776 6231
E   bearclaw@wxs.nl
W   www.absinthe.nl

Akinci [85]
Lijnbaansgracht 317
1017 WZ Amsterdam
T   638 0480
F   638 6485
E   info@akinci.nl
W   www.akinci.nl

Altmann [137]
Amsteldijk 25
1074 HS Amsterdam
T   662 7777
F   679 8952

Analik [161]
Hartenstraat 36
1016 CC Amsterdam
T   422 0561

E   info@analik.com
W   www.analik.com

Antonia by Yvette [58]
Gasthuismolensteeg 18–20
1016 AN Amsterdam
T   320 9443
F   622 3331
W   www.antoniabyyvette.nl

Art and Flowers [100]
KNSM-Laan 6
1019 LL Amsterdam
T/F 419 2273
E   art@euronet.nl
W   www.artandflowers.com

ArtBook [77]
Van Baerlestraat 126
1071 BD Amsterdam
T   664 0925
F   675 6290
E   info@artbook.nl
W   www.artbook.nl

Aziz [75]
Overtoom 259
1054 HW Amsterdam
T/F 616 1677
W   www.suite259.nl

Baby [17]
Nieuwezijds Voorburgwal 262
1012 RS Amsterdam

T   330 3202
W   www.joinbaby.com

Backstage [86]
Utrechtsedwarsstraat 67
1017 WC Amsterdam
T   622 3638

De Bakkerswinkel [132]
Warmoesstraat 69
1012 HX Amsterdam
T   489 8000
F   489 7878
W   www.debakkerswinkel.nl

Bar ARC [147]
Reguliersdwarsstraat 44
1017 BM Amsterdam
T   689 7070
F   689 7212
W   www.bararc.com

BEP [17]
Nieuwezijds Voorburgwal 260
1012 RS Amsterdam
T   626 5649
F   778 0123

Blaine's B&B at the Park [112]
Gerard Brandstraat 14hs
1054 JK Amsterdam
T   489 4958
E   blainesadam@chello.nl
W   www.blainesamsterdam.com

Blakes [120]
Keizersgracht 384
1016 GB Amsterdam
T   530 2010
F   530 2030
E   hotel@blakes.nl
W   www.blakesamsterdam.com

't Blauwe Theehuis [75]
Vondelpark 5
1071 AA Amsterdam
T   662 0254
F   670 9787
E   info@blauwetheehuis.nl
W   www.blauwetheehuis.nl

Blender [125]
Van der Palmkade 16
1051 RE Amsterdam
T   486 9860
F   486 9851
E   info@blender2003.com
W   www.blender2003.com

BLGK [52]
Hartenstraat 28
1016 CC Amsterdam
T   624 8154
F   625 7694

De Blonde Hollander [131]
Leidsekruisstraat 28
1017 RJ Amsterdam
T   627 0522

E info@deblondehollander.nl
W www.deblondehollander.nl

Bond [75]
Valeriusstraat 128–B
1075 GD Amsterdam
T 676 4647
F 379 0139

Bordewijk [40]
Noordermarkt 7
1015 MV Amsterdam
T 624 3899

Brasserie Bark [76]
Van Baerlestraat 120
1071 DB Amsterdam
T 675 0210
F 664 4207
E bark@cable.A2000.nl
W www.bark.nl

**Buffet van Odette
& Yvette** [58]
Herengracht 309
1016 AV Amsterdam
T 423 6034

Butler's [57]
Runstraat 22
1016 GK Amsterdam
T 676 4760
F 626 2158

Café 't Hoekje [22]
Krom Boomssloot 47
1011 GR Amsterdam
T 622 8131

Café de Jaren [134]
Nieuwe Doelenstraat 20–22
1012 CP Amsterdam
T 625 5771
F 624 0801
W www.cafe-de-jaren.nl

Café 't Papeneiland [144]
Prinsengracht 2
1015 DV Amsterdam
T 624 1989

**Café-Restaurant
Amsterdam** [128]
Watertorenplein 6
1015 PA Amsterdam
T 682 2667
F 682 2665
E mail@cradam.nl
W www.cradam.nl

Café 't Smalle [40]
Egelantiersgracht 12
1015 RL Amsterdam
T 623 9617

Café Tabac [40]
Brouwersgracht 101
1015 GC Amsterdam
T 622 4413

Canal House Hotel [114]
Keizersgracht 148
1015 CX Amsterdam
T 622 5182
F 624 1317
E info@canalhouse.nl
W www.canalhouse.nl

De Cantine [96]
Rietlandpark 373
1019 EM Amsterdam
T 419 4433

Capsicum [19]
Oude Hoogstraat 1
1012 CD Amsterdam
T 623 1016
W www.capsicumtextiles.com

Cellarrich [43]
Haarlemmerdijk 98
1013 JG Amsterdam
T 626 5526
F 427 0183
E bags@cellarrich.nl
W www.cellarrich.nl

Christian Best [54]
Keizersgracht 357
1016 EJ Amsterdam
T 623 2736

Christophe [137]
Leliegracht 46
1015 DH Amsterdam
T 625 0807
F 638 9132
E info@christophe.nl
W www.christophe.nl

Cineac [82]
Reguliersbreestraat 31
1017 CM Amsterdam

Cobra [75]
Hobbemastraat 18 /
Museumplein
1071 ZB Amsterdam
T 470 0111
F 470 0114
W www.cobracafe.com

The College Hotel [72]
Roelof Hartstraat 1
1071 VE Amsterdam

Collette van Landuijt [63]
Keizersgracht 476
1017 EG Amsterdam
T 622 2205

Cortina Papier [58]
Reestraat 22
1016 DN Amsterdam
T 623 6676
F 625 8698
E info@cortinapapier.nl
W www.cortinapapier.nl

Crust and Crumbs [44]
Haarlemmerstraat 108
1013 EW Amsterdam
T 528 6430
F 528 6431
E bread@crustandcrumbs.nl
W www.crustandcrumbs.nl

Dekker Antiquairs [67]
Spiegelgracht 9
1017 JP Amsterdam
T 623 8992
F 420 2112
E dekkerfa@xs4all.nl

Delores [17]
Nieuwezijds Voorburgwal
(opposite 289)
1012 Amsterdam
T 620 3302

Diep Venue [17]
Nieuwezijds Voorburgwal 256
1012 RS Amsterdam
T 420 2020

Dominio [100]
KNSM-Laan 301
1019 LE Amsterdam
T 419 0546
F 419 0547
W www.dominio.nl

DOTShop [39]
Haarlemmerdijk 71
1013 KC Amsterdam
T 612 4030

Droog & Co [154]
Rusland 3
1012 CK Amsterdam
T 626 9809
F 638 8828
E info@droogdesign.nl
W www.droogdesign.nl

Eduard Kramer [67]
Nieuwe Spiegelstraat 64
1017 DH Amsterdam
T 623 0832
F 638 8740
W www.antique-tileshop.nl

Eetcafe van Beeren [25]
Koningsstraat 54
1011 EW Amsterdam
T 622 2329

De Engel [90]
Albert Cuypstraat 182
1073 BL Amsterdam
T 675 0544
F 673 2196
E info.deengel@planet.nl
W www.de-engel.net

En Pluche [75]
Ruysdaelstraat 48

1071 XE Amsterdam
T 471 4695

Felix Meritis [60]
Keizersgracht 324
1016 EZ Amsterdam
T 626 2321
F 624 9368
E felix@felix.meritis.nl
W www.felix.meritis.nl

Finch [149]
Noordermarkt 5
1015 MV Amsterdam
T 626 2461

Fishes [89]
Utrechtsestraat 98
1017 VS Amsterdam
T 562 5252
W www.fishes.nl

**Fo Guang Shan 'He Hua'
Temple** [29]
Zeedijk 106–18
1012 BB Amsterdam
T 420 2357
F 420 4100
E IBPS@ibpsholland.demon.nl
W www.ibps.nl

Fred de la Bretonière [76]
Van Baerlestraat 34
1071 AX Amsterdam
T 470 9320
W www.bretoniere.nl

The Frozen Fountain [156]
Prinsengracht 629
1071 AX Amsterdam
T 622 9375
F 638 3041
E mail@frozenfountain.nl
W www.frozenfountain.nl

Galerie AHOI [96]
Oosterlijke Handelskade 999
1019 BW Amsterdam

Galerie Binnen [51]
Keizersgracht 82
1015 CT Amsterdam
T 625 9603
F 627 2654
E interno@xs4all.nl

Galerie Jos Art [96]
KNSM-Laan 291
1019 LE Amsterdam
T/F 418 7003
E josart@josart.nl
W www.josart.nl

Le Garage [75]
Ruysdaelstraat 54–56
1017 XE Amsterdam
T 679 7176

Gassan Diamonds [162]
Nieuwe Uilenburgerstraat 173–75
1011 LN Amsterdam
T   622 5333
F   624 6084
E   info@gassandiamonds.nl
W   www.gassandiamonds.nl

Geels & Co [26]
Warmoesstraat 67
1012 HX Amsterdam
T   624 0683
F   622 7276
E   info@geels.nl
W   www.geels.nl

Getto [26]
Warmoesstraat 51
1012 HW Amsterdam
T   421 5151
W   www.getto.nl

Hair & Body Affairs [98]
Levantkade 167
1019 MD Amsterdam
T   419 1951 (hair), 419 0354 (body)

Hester van Eeghen [52]
Hartenstraat 37 (bags)
1016 CA Amsterdam
T   626 9212
Hartenstraat 1 (shoes)
1016 BZ Amsterdam
T   626 9211
F   626 9213
E   info@hestervaneeghen.com
W   www.hestervaneeghen.com

H.J. van de Kerkhof [52]
Wolvenstraat 9–11
1016 EM Amsterdam
T   623 4666
F   620 2223
E   kerkhof@wirehub.nl

De Hollandsche Manege [72]
Vondelstraat 140
1054 GT Amsterdam
T   618 0942
E   dehollandschemanege@
    hotmail.com
W   www.dehollandschemanege.nl

Hortus Botanicus [90]
Plantage Middenlaan 2a
1018 DD Amsterdam
T   625 8411
F   625 7006
E   info@dehortus.nl
W   www.hortus-botanicus.nl

Hotel Arena [108]
's-Gravesandestraat 51
1092 AA Amsterdam
T   850 2400
F   850 2415
E   info@hotelarena.nl
W   www.hotelarena.nl

Hotel Jan Luyken [110]
Jan Luijkenstraat 58
1071 CS Amsterdam
T   573 0730
F   676 3841
E   jan-luyken@bilderberg.nl
W   www.janluyken.nl

Hotel V [118]
Victorieplein 42
1078 PH Amsterdam
T   662 3233
F   676 6398
E   stay@hotelv.nl
W   www.hotelv.nl

Huis Marseille [63]
Keizersgracht 401
1016 EK Amsterdam
T   531 8989
F   531 8988
E   info@huismarseille.nl
W   www.huismarseille.nl

In 't Aepjen [140]
Zeedijk 1
1012 AN Amsterdam
T   626 8401

In de Waag [22]
Nieuwmarkt 4
1012 CR Amsterdam
T   422 7772
F   422 8641
E   info@indewaag.nl
W   www.indewaag.nl

Inez IPSC [124]
Amstel 2
1017 AA Amsterdam
T   639 2899

Innerspace [20]
Staalstraat 5
1011 JJ Amsterdam
T/F 320 0064
E   staalstraat@innerspace.nl
W   www.innerspace.nl

Jacob Hooy & Co [29]
Kloveniersburgwal 12
1012 CT Amsterdam
T   624 3041
E   info@jacobhooy.nl
W   www.jacobhooy.nl

JAN [86]
Utrechtsestraat 74
1017 VR Amsterdam
T   626 4301
E   jan.amsterdam@planet.nl

J.G. Beune [45]
Haarlemmerdijk 156–58
1013 JJ Amsterdam
T   624 8356

Jimmy Woo [67]
Korte Leidsedwarsstraat 16–18
1017 RC Amsterdam

Joe's Vliegerwinkel [19]
Nieuwe Hoogstraat 19
1011 HD Amsterdam
T   625 0139
W   www.joesvliegerwinkel.nl

Joia [148]
Korte Leidsedwarsstraat 45
1017 PW Amsterdam
T   626 6769
E   joia@diningcity.nl

JOOT [157]
Hartenstraat 15
1016 BZ Amsterdam
T   688 1783
E   info@joot.nl
W   www.joot.nl

Juggle Store [21]
Staalstraat 3
1011 JJ Amsterdam
T   420 1980
F   428 4740
E   shop@juggle-store.com
W   www.juggle-store.com

De Kaaskamer [57]
Runstraat 7
1016 GJ Amsterdam
T/F 623 3483

Kanis & Meiland [100]
Levantkade 127
1019 MJ Amsterdam
T   418 2439
W   www.kanisenmeiland.nl

Kapitein Zeppos [145]
Gebed Zonder End 5
1012 HS Amsterdam
T   624 2057
F   639 2528
E   info@kapiteinzeppos.nl
W   www.zeppos.nl

De Kas [136]
Kamerlingh Onneslaan 3
1097 DE Amsterdam
T   462 4562
F   462 4563
E   info@restaurantdekas.nl
W   www.restaurantdekas.nl

Keet in Huis [99]
KNSM-Laan 303
1019 LE Amsterdam
T   419 5958
E   info@keetinhius.nl
W   www.keetinhuis.nl

Kitsch [89]
Utrechtsestraat 42
1017 VP Amsterdam
T   625 9251

F   622 1016
W   www.restaurant-kitsch.nl

Kitsch Kitchen [51]
Rozengracht 8–12
1016 NB Amsterdam
T   622 8261
F   320 1718
E   supermercado@
    kitschkitchen.nl
W   www.kitschkitchen.nl

Klamboe Unlimited [51]
Prinsengracht 232
1016 HE Amsterdam
T   622 9492
F   620 6358
E   info@klamboe-unlimited.com
W   www.klamboe.com

Knuffels [31]
Sint Antoniesbreestraat 39–51
1011 HB Amsterdam
T   623 0632
W   www.knuffels.com

Koan Float [63]
Herengracht 321
1016 AW Amsterdam
T   555 0333
F   555 0377
E   info@koan-float.com
W   www.koan-float.com

De Kookboekhandel [57]
Runstraat 26
1016 GK Amsterdam
T   622 4768
F   638 1088
E   info@kookboekhandel.com
W   www.kookboekhandel.com

Lairesse Apotheek [167]
De Lairessestraat 40 huis
1071 PB Amsterdam
T   662 1022
F   671 3660
W   www.delairesseapotheek.nl

Lambiek [64]
Kerkstraat 119
1017 GE Amsterdam
T   626 7543
F   620 6372
E   lambiek@lambiek.net
W   www.lambiek.net

Latei [22]
Zeedijk 143
1012 AW Amsterdam
T   625 7485

Laundry Industry [17]
Spuistraat 137 (Magna Plaza)
1012 SV Amsterdam
T   625 3960
W   www.laundryindustry.com

Liesbeth Royaards [51]
Herengracht 70b
1015 BR Amsterdam
T   626 5026

Lime [25]
Zeedijk 104
1021 BB Amsterdam
T   639 3020

Lloyd Hotel [96]
Oostelijke Handelskade 34
1019 BN Amsterdam
T   419 1840
E   post@lloydhotel.nl
W   www.lloydhotel.nl

LOF [44]
Haarlemmerstraat 62
1013 ES Amsterdam
T   620 2997

Lokaal 't Loosje [25]
Nieuwmarkt 32–34
1012 CS Amsterdam
T   627 2635

Lust [58]
Runstraat 13
1016 GJ Amsterdam
T   626 5791
E   info@lustamsterdam.nl
W   www.lustamsterdam.nl

Madame Jeanette [146]
1e van der Helststraat 42
1072 NV Amsterdam
T   673 3332

Mamouche [127]
Quellijnstraat 104
1072 XZ Amsterdam
T   673 6361

**Mart Visser
Haute Couture** [77]
Paulus Potterstraat 30a
1071 DA Amsterdam
T   571 2020
F   670 3714
E   info@martvisser.nl
W   www.martvisser.nl

MasAntiek & Décor [45]
Haarlemmerstraat 25
1013 EJ Amsterdam
T   422 7100
F   422 7130

Meeuwig & Zn [163]
Haarlemmerstraat 70
1013 ET Amsterdam
T   626 5286
E   info@meeuwig.nl
W   www.meeuwig.nl

Mendo [55]
Berenstraat 11

1016 GG Amsterdam
T   612 1216
F   612 6229
E   contact@mendo.nl
W   www.mendo.nl

Menno Kroon [158]
Cornelis Schuytstraat 11
1071 JC Amsterdam
T   679 1950
F   672 1935
E   info@mennokroon.nl
W   www.mennokroon.nl

Metri [26]
Koningsstraat 36
1011 EW Amsterdam
T   627 5318
F   422 3063

Metz & Co [63]
Leidsestraat 34–36
1017 PB Amsterdam
T   520 7020

Moko [126]
Amstelveld 12
1017 JD Amsterdam
T   626 1199
F   626 6059
E   facemoko@zonnet.nl

Morlang [142]
Keizersgracht 451
1017 DK Amsterdam
T   625 2681
E   mail@morlang.nl
W   www.morlang.nl

Museum Amstelkring [29]
Oudezijds Voorburgwal 40
1012GE Amsterdam
T   624 6604
F   638 1822
E   info@museumamstelkring.nl
W   www.museumamstelkring.nl

Museum van Loon [85]
Keizersgracht 672
1017 ET Amsterdam
T   624 5255
W   www.museumvanloon.nl

**Museum Willet-
Holthuysen** [85]
Herengracht 605
1017 CE Amsterdam
T   523 1822
F   620 7789
E   info@willetholthuysen.
    amsterdam.nl
W   www.willetholthuysen.nl

NeMo Science Museum [90]
Oosterdok 2
1011 VX Amsterdam
T   0900 9191 100
F   531 3535
W   www.e-nemo.nl

New Deli [135]
Haarlemmerstraat 73
1013 AL Amsterdam
T   626 2755
F   427 8170
E   info@newdeli.nl
W   www.newdeli.nl

Nijhof & Lee [21]
Staalstraat 13a
1011 JK Amsterdam
T   620 3980
F   639 3294
E   nijlee@xs4all.nl
W   www.nijhoflee.nl

The Nijntje Shop [77]
Beethovenstraat 71
1077 HP Amsterdam
T   671 9707
W   www.nijntje.nl

NL Lounge [17]
Nieuwezijds Voorburgwal 169
1012 RK Amsterdam
T/F 622 7510
E   info@nieuwezijdslounge.nl
W   www.nieuwezijdslounge.nl

Nomads [150]
Rozengracht 133 I
1016 LV Amsterdam
T   344 6401
F   344 6405
E   info@restaurantnomads.nl
W   www.restaurantnomads.nl

De Oceaan [99]
R.J.H. Fortuynplein 29
(Borneokade)
1019 WL Amsterdam
T   419 0020
W   www.oceaan.nl

De Ode [98]
Levantkade 51
1019 MJ Amsterdam
T   419 0882
F   419 2409
E   ode@uitvaart.nl
W   www.uitvaart.nl/ode

Odessa [131]
Veemkade 259
1019 CZ Amsterdam
T   419 3010
F   419 3011
E   info@de-odessa.nl
W   www.de-odessa.nl

Ozenfant [54]
Huidenstraat 3–5
1016 ER Amsterdam
T   638 2957
F   638 8977
E   info@ozenfant.com
W   ozenfant.com

Pakhuis Amsterdam [156]
Oostelijke Handelskade 17
1019 BL Amsterdam
T   421 1033
F   627 5158
W   www.pakhuisamsterdam.nl

Panama [150]
Oostelijke Handelskade 4
1019 BM Amsterdam
T   311 8686
F   311 8681
E   info@panama.nl
W   www.panama.nl

Parisienne [55]
Berenstraat 4
1016 GH Amsterdam
T   428 0834

Paul Warmer [160]
Leidsestraat 41
1017 NV Amsterdam
T   427 8011
E   paul@paulwarmer.com

PGC Hajenius [162]
Rokin 92–96
1012 KZ Amsterdam
T   625 9985
W   www.hajenius.com

Pilat & Pilat [155]
KNSM-Laan 19
1019 LA Amsterdam
T   419 3670
F   419 3675
E   ppa@pilat.nl
W   www.pilat.pilat.nl

Plancius [143]
Plantage Kerklaan 61a
1018 CX Amsterdam
T   330 9469

De Plantage [89]
Utrechtsestraat 130
1017 VT Amsterdam
T   626 4684

Pol's Potten [100]
KNSM-Laan 39
1019 LA Amsterdam
T   419 3541
F   362 8838
E   info.online@polspotten.nl
W   www.polspotten.nl

Pompadour [132]
Huidenstraat 12
1016 ES Amsterdam
T   623 9554
F   659 3414

Possen.com [161]
Van Baerlestraat 39
1071 AP Amsterdam
T   471 2050
W   www.possen.com

Puccini Bomboni [164]
Staalstraat 17
1011 JK Amsterdam
T   626 5474
F   422 9709
E   info@puccinibomboni.com
W   www.puccinibomboni.com

Puck [18]
Nieuwe Hoogstraat 1a
1011 HC Amsterdam
T   625 4201

Pygma-Lion [129]
Nieuwe Spiegelstraat 5a
1017 DB Amsterdam
T   420 7022
W   www.pygma-lion.com

**Reflex Modern Art
Gallery** [64]
Weteringschans 79
1017 RX Amsterdam
T   627 2832
F   620 2590
W   www.reflex-art.nl

Restaurant Blue Pepper [39]
Nassaukade 366
1054 AD Amsterdam
T   489 7039

De Ridder [155]
Hartenstraat 21–27
1016 CA Amsterdam
T   623 1180
F   623 7488
E   info@de-ridder.nl
W   www.de-ridder.nl

Rusland [21]
Rusland 14–16
1012 CL Amsterdam
T   627 9468

Sauna Deco [51]
Herengracht 115
1015 BE Amsterdam
T   623 8215
F   627 1773
W   www.saunadeco.nl

La Savonnerie [61]
Prinsengracht 294
1016 HJ Amsterdam
T   428 1139
F   428 0323
E   info@savonnerie.nl
W   www.savonnerie.nl

SBK Amsterdam [100]
KNSM-Laan 307–9
1019 LE Amsterdam
T   620 1321
F   418 2866
E   knsm@sbk.nl
W   www.sbk.nl

Seeds of Passion [86]
Utrechtsestraat 26
1017 VN Amsterdam
T   625 1100
E   ams@seedsofpassion.nl
W   www.seedsofpassion.nl

Seven One Seven [106]
Prinsengracht 717
1017 JW Amsterdam
T   427 0717
F   423 0717
E   info@717hotel.nl
W   www.717hotel.nl

The Shirt Shop [61]
Reguliersdwarsstraat 64
1017 BM Amsterdam
T   423 2088

Shoebaloo [159]
P.C. Hooftstraat 80
1071 CB Amsterdam
T   671 2210

Skins [57]
Runstraat 9
1016 GJ Amsterdam
T   528 6922
F   528 6921
E   info@skins.nl
W   www.skins.nl

SM Bureau Amsterdam [39]
Rozenstraat 59
1016 NN Amsterdam
T   422 0471
F   626 1730
W   www.smba.nl

Spring [136]
Willemsparkweg 177
1071 GZ Amsterdam
T   675 4421
F   676 9414
E   info@restaurantspring.nl
W   www.restaurantspring.nl

Stedelijk Museum [72]
Paulus Potterstraat 13
1071 CX Amsterdam
T   573 2737
F   675 2716
W   www.stedelijk.nl

De Still [141]
Spuistraat 326
1012 VX Amsterdam
T   427 6809
W   www.destill.nl

Suite [146]
Sint Nicolaasstraat 43
1012 NJ Amsterdam
T   489 6531
F   775 0505
E   suite@chello.nl

Supperclub [151]
Jonge Roelensteeg 21
1012 PL Amsterdam
T   344 6400
F   344 6405
E   info@supperclub.nl
W   www.supperclub.com

De Taart van m'n Tante [133]
1e Jacob van Campenstraat 35
1072 BC Amsterdam
T   776 4600
F   776 4604
E   info@detaart.nl
W   www.detaart.nl

TamTam [51]
Prinsengracht 381
1016 HL Amsterdam
T   612 1005
F   428 0614

Tempo Doeloe [130]
Utrechtsestraat 75
1017 VJ Amsterdam
T   625 6718
W   www.tempodoeloe
     restaurant.nl

Theater Tuschinski [82]
Reguliersbreestraat 26–34
1017 CN Amsterdam
T   0900 1458
W   www.pathe.nl/tuschinski

Tike Design [31]
Grimburgwal 15
1012 GA Amsterdam
T   428 8510
E   tikedesign@zonnet.nl
W   www.tikedesign.com

TinkerBell [64]
Spiegelgracht 10–12
1017 JR Amsterdam
T   625 8830
E   info@tinkerbelltoys.nl
W   www.tinkerbelltoys.nl

Torch [39]
Lauriergracht 94
1016 RN Amsterdam
T   626 0284
F   623 8892
E   mail@torchgallery.com
W   www.torchgallery.com

Unlimited Delicious [165]
Haarlemmerstraat 122
1013 EX Amsterdam
T   622 4829
F   528 7034
E   keesraat@
     unlimiteddelicious.nl
W   www.unlimiteddelicious.nl

Vakzuid [128]
Olympisch Stadion 35
1076 DE Amsterdam
T   570 8400
F   570 8410
E   info@vakzuid.nl
W   www.vakzuid.nl

Van Gogh Museum [72]
Paulus Potterstraat 7
1071 CX Amsterdam
T   570 5252
F   570 5222
E   info@vangoghmuseum.nl
W   www.vangoghmuseum.nl

Van Ravenstein [159]
Keizersgracht 359 and
Huidenstraat
1016 EJ Amsterdam
T   639 0067
F   639 0322

Vivian Hann [157]
Haarlemmerdijk 102
1013 JG Amsterdam
T   06 22 04 94 65

De Vlieger [82]
Amstel 34–52
1017 AB Amsterdam
T   623 5834

Voorwerp [43]
Haarlemmerplein 13 hs
1013 HP Amsterdam
T   624 2686
F   622 0764
W   www.voorwerp.nl

W139 [26]
Warmoesstraat 139
1012 JB Amsterdam
T   622 9434
F   625 1226
E   info@w139.nl
W   www.w139.nl

Walem [144]
Keizersgracht 449
1017 DK Amsterdam
T   625 3544

De Waterwinkel [165]
Roelof Hartstraat 10
1071 VH Amsterdam
T   675 5932

Westergasfabriek [37]
Haarlemmerweg 8–10
1014 BE Amsterdam
T   586 0710
F   681 3062
E   info@westergasfabriek.nl
W   www.westergasfabriek.nl